CW00469561

Funerals Your Way

A person-centred approach to planning a funeral

Sarah Jones

Sarah Jones

Legal Disclaimer:

Family and Friend quotes have been paraphrased.
Any "thoughts" contained or referenced throughout this
book belong to the author Sarah Jones.

Table of Contents

Appendices

Chapter 1

Setting the scene

Who is this book for?

It is almost certain that every one of us will attend, arrange and participate in numerous funerals throughout our lives. Many people face these experiences with little prior knowledge and that means that it can be a bewildering and disempowering time.

This book is designed to create a guided space for you to make real choices without feeling overwhelmed.

With some simple information, a step-by-step guide and a little preparation, you will feel more confident, less vulnerable and more in control. Everyone experiences bereavement in their own personal way but with the right support we can find the resilience that is inside us all.

If you know a little about the funeral arrangement process and the possibilities available to you, it will enable you to create a funeral that truly reflects the person who has died and it is likely to be helpful for you and your friends and family.

Whether you are preparing yourself because someone you are close to has a life-limiting condition, or you have already found yourself involved in making funeral arrangements, this short book will turn something apparently overwhelming into a manageable set of decisions for you to consider.

It will help you to make sure that you can get what you need from the arrangement process and from the funeral itself.

Even if you are not directly involved in the funeral arrangements, you may be providing support to someone who is more closely involved. With a sound knowledge base, you can make insightful suggestions and help them to consider the choices that are available to them.

The concepts, options and ideas considered in the book are equally helpful if you are considering your own funeral, or if you would like to talk to someone about what their funeral wishes might be.

A little knowledge allows us to open the door to this dialogue and can result in some very powerful and positive conversations with those close to us.

In my experience, after someone has died, people find it very helpful if they know something of the person's funeral wishes. Whether these are just one or two headline instructions, or a very detailed plan, doesn't matter – just knowing where to start is very reassuring.

With that in mind and regardless of your age and fitness, when you reach the end of this book, I would encourage you to write down one or two thoughts about your own funeral and put them somewhere safe.

How to use this book

I suggest that you initially read through the book from start to finish and then refer to any chapters that you would like to look at again. The first few chapters will help you to gather your thoughts, which will inform the choices that you make throughout the rest of the arrangements.

At the end of each chapter, you can write down a few thoughts and reflections, and I would encourage you to do so because they will be helpful to refer to later.

This book is designed to help people who are intending to use the support of a funeral director. However, this is not essential and if you would like to plan a funeral without engaging the services of a funeral director, then there are various other books and online resources that you might find helpful.

Choosing a funeral director

A funeral director is someone who will collect the body of the person who has died and care for them until the committal (burial or cremation) takes place.

They will also support you to understand your options, make the necessary arrangements and will then be present to "direct" the funeral on the day that it takes place.

Choosing a funeral director is a very important decision and a key first step in the process. Like all service providers, different funeral directors have different approaches and ways of working.

Having a personal connection with a company or person can be very reassuring, but to make sure that you find someone who best meets your needs you may want to ask them some short questions before making your final choice.

You might consider asking them how they might help you and how they would describe their approach. You might ask who will be supporting you, and whether it will be the same person throughout the arrangement and at the funeral itself – having this continuity might be reassuring for you later.

Some funeral directors have several small high street premises and a separate central hub where they look after the person who has died.

If it feels important to know where the funeral director will be looking after your relative or friend, and who will be providing any personal care, then you could ask them this question before making your final choice.

Funerals can be very expensive, and many people are unsure how funeral costs are broken down or how much individual items cost.

Whether price is at the forefront of your mind or not, I would suggest that it is important to know how much things cost before making your choices. So, you might want to check that a specific funeral director has their prices readily and transparently available.

It is intended that this book would be helpful regardless of who you are planning the funeral for. Some people suggest that the approach to the funeral would be different depending on the age or the circumstances in which someone has died.

I believe that so long as you put the person's and your needs at the centre of the arrangement process the rest will follow. A person-centred approach will mean that anyone faced with the prospect of having to plan a funeral will create something that is right for them.

Please use the boxes below to write down a few of your thoughts.

Regarding the funeral that you are considering, what are your priorities at the moment?

Is there anything that you are worried about?

Chapter 2

Where to start

Start with the person themselves

When you are thinking about a funeral, the best place to start is by thinking about the person themselves.

Before you start to take any action, or make any decisions, taking five minutes to reflect on the person themselves and their lives will help to inform all the choices that you make thereafter, and make the funeral truly reflect them as an individual.

So, what is important to them? Are there any principles that they live their lives by? For example, a love of nature or the environment? Are they a quiet and private person, or do they prefer big social gatherings and spending time with many different people?

"She fiercely loved her family and although she was known and liked by many people she was actually very private."

"She lived life to the full and always celebrated every occasion to the max. She loved a party and enjoyed being the centre of attention – although her life was too short, she certainly packed as much in as she possibly could".

"He was very organised, neat and tidy and liked things to be just-so. He believed that we shouldn't be wasteful and should try to leave the world in the same state that we found it in."

If they work, what do they do? Is this an important part of their lives that might be reflected somewhere in the funeral? Or is it a way to make money to fund their hobbies and support their families? If they spent time in military service, is that something that might be reflected in the service, or would you prefer that this be less visually prominent?

"He spent some time in the armed forces when he was a young man but that was a long time ago. It was something that he was very proud of but I don't want that to be the only part of his life that the funeral pays tribute to."

What do they enjoy doing in their free time? Do they have any hobbies, or are they a member of any groups that give them great pleasure?

Are there any places that are special to them? If they are an active member of the local church, golf club, bridge club or cycling group, these may all be mentioned or featured during the funeral.

Is music important? For some people, this is a very important part of their lives whereas for others, it may be less significant.

"She organised a lot of events at the local school, and when she was well she really enjoyed playing tennis and bowls in the village."

"His death was so sudden and unexpected, and it had a big impact on all the people at his school. We knew that some of the service needed to take place there because the whole community needed the opportunity to say Goodbye."

Are there any objects or places that you immediately associate with them? For example, do they never go anywhere without a specific shopping bag, newspaper or the *Racing Times*? Or do they always have a particular sweet available to give to everyone they meet?

Are they always sitting next to their knitting basket, or have they made something that they are particularly proud of (like a painting), or are they known far and wide for their coffee cake?

Are they known for growing vegetables and prize dahlias? Do they always have a vase of sunflowers on the kitchen table?

"She had a bowl of boiled sweets at the front door and always offered everyone one as they came in or left the house. I'm not sure that she ever ate one herself but it seemed to mean a lot to her for us to take and enjoy one."

An arrangement including vegetables for a man who loved to grow his own

Who is important to them? Are they primarily focussed on their families, or do they have a small or larger group of friends? Recognising these people at this point means that you might see opportunities for them to participate in, or contribute to, the funeral.

Maybe a close friend could be invited to bring some decorations for the tables during refreshments or is an expert at photography and could be asked if they have some nice photographs to be included in a display.

If they are a member of a choir, could they lead any singing during the service?

"Her oldest grandchild plays the flute and she used to love to hear her play. We didn't want to put any pressure on her, but she seemed really keen to play at the funeral. She played Twinkle Twinkle Little Star and it was perfect."

Some people have lived more adventurous lives than others, and no one has led a life without some challenges and difficult times and relationships. Some recollections might not be entirely positive and uplifting and please be reassured that this is the reality for most people. Do you want the funeral to focus on the positive reflections only, or would you also like to acknowledge some of the more challenging times and traits?

"My dad was not the easiest of men and I wanted everyone present at the funeral to feel that the service was true and honest. Full of great memories, but also respectfully recognising that some things were a little less easy for us all."

"For me, the funeral should be about all the happy times and celebrating a very special life. I want to recognise the amazing woman she was and everything that she achieved in her life."

Once you have spent some time considering these questions, and any others that feel relevant to you, then they can inform the decisions that you need to make during the arrangements.

Much of this may be captured in the words that are spoken but there are also other means for them to be included in gentle and personal ways.

For example, for someone who was a life-long supporter of the Royal Society for the Protection of Birds you might include a small decorative bird in the flower arrangement, or you might choose for donations to be made to this charity in their memory.

If they were a postman or lollipop lady, their hat could be included on top of the coffin. Their certificates, drawings, paintings or cycling jersey might be positioned for people to admire during refreshments.

A precious book, bottle of whisky, teddy bear or well-worn walking boots could be placed on a small table at the front of the room during a service.

A flag might be present on the coffin, or elsewhere, and if there was somewhere that they loved to go for a meal or a drink, maybe part of the funeral could take place there.

While for many people this thought process may be very empowering and helpful, others might not be willing or able to engage in this way. Please don't feel any pressure to do so. There is no right or wrong way to plan a funeral and you should not feel compelled to personalise the process or service if this not something that you want.

What do you already know?

Next, it is helpful to consider whether you are aware of any formal instructions that have been left. Sometimes these can be included as part of a Will, or they may have been documented separately as a Funeral Wishes Document.

When someone has purchased a pre-paid funeral plan, these may sometimes also include some personal instructions, but not always.

"She knew that she was going to die, and she made sure that we knew exactly what she wanted. She seemed to find it reassuring that her funeral would be as she wanted it to be. She had instructed certain people about what they were to say and we even knew that there were to be balloons and a popcorn machine for the children."

Do you remember any informal comments or reflections that the person shared with you?

Sometimes, people make positive or negative comments when watching a funeral on the television or after they have attended or planned a funeral themselves.

It may also be worth asking people who are close to them if they if they have any recollections that can give you a steer at this time.

"After we planned Grandpa's funeral together, Grandma said that she wanted the same except she chose a different hymn and told us the flowers that she wanted."

It would also be helpful for you to reflect on your own ideas about what you think may or may not be helpful as part of the funeral service.

It's likely that your thoughts will evolve on this through the funeral arranging process but if you have any thoughts now, it might be helpful to have them written down.

For example, if you have attended a funeral that you found particularly meaningful, what was it that you felt you had made a connection with? Or in contrast, have you had some experiences that you have found less positive? Sometimes knowing what you don't want is just as powerful as starting to think about what you do want.

"I went to a funeral where the service didn't seem to mention the person who had died at all. I could have been at anyone's funeral and there was nothing personal about it. I want the service to be all about him."

The tone of the funeral

Giving consideration to the tone that you would like to create can be helpful at this point. Would you prefer for the funeral to be simple and understated or more elaborate?

Would you like for any part of the funeral to be private or will all aspects of the funeral be open to everybody?

Are you acknowledging the life and loss in a serious, more formal way, or would you prefer the funeral to be more uplifting and encourage people to smile and laugh?

It is always possible for the same funeral to have different parts, with a different tone or atmosphere to each. For example, a more formal funeral service could be followed by a more uplifting, celebratory gathering thereafter.

"He told us to not make any fuss! So, we created a funeral that we thought was nice and respectful but kept in mind that we

needed to keep it simple and respect his wishes."

"She was a bit of a diva and liked to be the centre of attention. She told us she didn't want anything sad and we decided to throw a massive party for everyone to celebrate her and each other."

"Because he died before he was born it was really important that people recognised how much we loved him. We wanted everyone to know about him and for the whole community to see how important he was."

"We consciously decided that we wanted the time at the crematorium to be for us to be able to be honest about how sad we were that she had died. We then wanted the time afterwards to really celebrate how much she had touched our lives and for that to be filled with laughter and banter."

When you have decided the tone that you feel is most appropriate to your circumstances, this might help you to decide what language is appropriate for the occasion.

For example, you might choose to simply call the gathering a "Funeral Service" or you might wish to call it "A Service to Celebrate the Life of …" or "A Service of Thanksgiving for …".

To some people these nuances in language are not important, but to others they are a helpful way to indicate the tone that you are creating and give a signal to people attending about the way that you would like them to personally frame and engage in the service.

Recognising the existence of significant others

People have different opinions about who a funeral is for. Some people feel strongly that the funeral should only reflect the wishes and choices of the person who has died. In contrast, others would argue that the funeral should focus more on meeting the needs of family and close friends.

Some feel strongly that individual members of a larger community will also need the funeral to enable them to acknowledge that someone has died. In practice, it is often possible to achieve a balance between all of these objectives.

It is likely that there will be several different people who will be experiencing a significant loss because of the bereavement.

This may include close family members but could also be friends or more distant relatives. I would encourage you to spend a few minutes to think about who these people might be.

It may be that only one or two people have direct involvement in planning with the funeral director but acknowledging who the other significant people are at this time may help you to consider their perspective in key aspects of the arrangement.

Deciding who will meet the funeral director is likely to depend on where people live, competing commitments and personalities and relationships. Some people find it helpful if they are involved or can participate in some way too.

However, particularly if the person who has died has touched many lives, this has to be managed in a way that is constructive and positive.

It is likely that a small number of people will be involved throughout the decision-making process and that other people are invited to contribute with more specific decisions or tasks which play to their specific strengths.

For example, recruiting the help of a creative family member to design a written order of service may be very helpful to you and a great honour for them. Asking close friends to contribute some reflections to be shared in a eulogy is likely to be a powerful way for them to participate and acknowledges their presence in the person's life.

It is very usual for different people within the same family or any other group to have different opinions on what may be most appropriate or what they find to be most meaningful.

This can on occasion lead to conflict while planning a funeral. However, if everyone can be encouraged to see that a funeral serves to meet the needs of several different people, that can help to set the scene for working together more collaboratively.

With careful planning and consideration, a funeral can be created to include enough of what everyone needs for it to be helpful to those that matter.

One of the benefits of involving and proactively informing people about certain choices is that, if they have a better understanding of what to expect and why those decisions have been made, they are more likely to feel more able to engage with the funeral in a meaningful way.

If there are people for whom a particular choice may be difficult, it is likely to be helpful for them to understand why the decision was made.

For example, if the person who has died has requested a predominately non-religious service then there may be some members of the family for whom that would not be their preference, but they may be more likely to respect the decision if they appreciate that it was made by the person themselves.

Please use the boxes below to write down a few of your thoughts.

What do you know about their wishes?

Who are people who are significant to
consider, include or manage sensitively?

What do you know about what you
would like, or would not find helpful?

Chapter Three

Beliefs and rituals

Religion and belief

First and foremost in many people's minds is whether religion will play a part in the funeral or not. Sometimes the answer to this question feels immediately clear.

For example, if someone has been a life-long church attender and would describe themselves as Christian it is likely that their faith will be a fundamental part of the funeral.

In contrast some people actively express that they do not want religion to be part of the ceremony in any way, or they may never have expressed any connection with any faith.

However, the situation can often be slightly less clear. Someone may have attended church regularly as a child, but it may have been a less prominent part of their later lives.

Other people describe themselves as Christian but choose not to attend church and express their beliefs in their own personal way.

"He hadn't been to church for a very long time but said he was a Christian when anyone asked him. We decided to have the funeral in church but made sure that other parts of his life and personality were included in the service."

Increasingly people are describing themselves as spiritual, rather than religious, basing their ideas on various philosophical principles rather than on a named religion or church. Many have also extended a more flexible interpretation to various religions and the boundaries between religion and culture seem to be becoming increasingly blurred.

For example, someone may feel a close affinity to a church building, seeing it as the most beautiful and significant location within their community, but may not describe themselves as Christian.

Others may feel a close connection to a hymn because it was significant at some point in their lives, such as at their wedding, but may not describe themselves as Christian.

Furthermore, someone may identify closely with key principles from different religions and members of the same family and close friendship group might actively engage with very different faiths.

It is possible to have a full traditional religious service, no religious content at all and everything in between. A funeral can include as much or as little religion or spirituality as you feel is most appropriate. It may even include open acknowledgement that the people present may have different interpretations of the purpose and meaning of life and what happens thereafter.

"He told me that he didn't want a religious service but I know that is very difficult for his parents and sister. We found a way to fulfil his wishes during the service but acknowledged that it was hard for them and made sure that they had the opportunity for prayer."

At this stage in the process I would suggest that the most important thing is for you to acknowledge the beliefs and practices of both the person who has died and the key people who will be attending.

Once this is clear in your mind then it will inform many of the decisions that you make thereafter.

Individual, family and group rituals

Ritual is a word that is commonly associated with funerals and funeral practices. I find it most helpful to think of a ritual as something that individuals or groups repeatedly do, and which helps them to connect with an event or each other. As a society, within families and as individuals, we identify with ritual on many different levels.

For example, many people light a candle in remembrance of someone who has died, football supporters may have a lucky item of clothing that they always wear to a match, or a gentleman may always buy his wife a rose on their wedding anniversary.

Family rituals and traditions may include opening one present on Christmas Eve, or a family gathering at a certain place at the same time of year for a specific reason.

Most religions are associated with certain funeral rituals. Again, you may find some of these very helpful and others less so.

You may also have identified that there are certain practices or choices that have consistently been made for funerals within your family and it may feel appropriate to repeat some of these choices in recognition of that connection.

For example, members of the family may come to see the person who has died at the family home or the funeral director's premises together, or place a certain flower on the coffin at the end of the service.

"Funerals seem to be the only time that our family get together nowadays. After the service we always get together, have a few drinks and it's a really nice opportunity to catch up with each other. It's a really positive part of the day."

If the person who has died was an active member of any groups during their life this may be something that you want to reflect as part of the funeral.

For example, if they served in the armed forces then there are some associated funeral rituals that you may consider. Standard bearers may be invited to be present, the Union Jack flag placed on the coffin and the "Last Post" could be played at the end of the service.

As a member of certain groups or a supporter of certain competitive sports teams, the rituals associated with them may have been particularly important to them and might have a place within the service.

"He was a very proud member of the darts team and his favourite set of darts were his pride and joy. We put a photo in his coffin of him with the team and placed his darts on the coffin during the service. It made us smile."

When you are considering this, you may find yourself thinking of many examples that seem relevant or you may conclude that rituals play a less significant part in your life.

The most important thing is to have had the thought process, to have had the opportunity to identify something that might be helpful.

Please use the boxes below to write down a few of your thoughts.

What do you know about the religious or spiritual beliefs of the person who the funeral is for?

Are there any personal, family or group rituals that you might consider including?

Chapter Four

The committal

What is the committal?

When people speak about a committal they are usually referring to one of two things.

They might either be talking about the final location where the body is placed (for example the grave) or they are referring to the final words spoken at the end of the funeral service.

This chapter considers the different committal types and locations available to you, whereas the words of committal will be discussed later in this book.

An important question when making funeral choices relates to what will finally happen to the body of the person who has died.

When deciding what you feel is most appropriate for the situation you are in there are several things that you might like to consider.

Has the person themselves ever expressed any preference about where they would like their body taking to?

Is there a certain tradition within your family that you would like to uphold? Is there anything that you feel you would find most comforting? Or do you find any of the options particularly challenging?

"Every family funeral has taken place at the local crematorium and Dad made it clear to us that he wanted the same. He never really told me much else about his wishes but just knowing that I was able to do the one thing that he asked meant a lot to me."

At the present time, your choice is essentially between burial or cremation. Choosing whether you prefer burial or cremation is an important part of the funeral arrangement process.

The answer to this question may be immediately obvious to you but if you feel less certain I would suggest you find out more about the options in your area.

There is no need to feel rushed into making this decision and it is likely with time it will become clear what the most fitting choice is.

Burial

Burials can take place in a number of locations and although there is a common misconception that there is very little burial space available it certainly remains a viable option.

Burials can take place in a church graveyard, local authority or privately-owned cemetery, woodland or natural burial ground. Some of these burial grounds will have a ceremony space on site, whereas others will not.

Local authority or privately-owned cemeteries may be located on the same grounds as a crematorium and they often have neat rows of headstones to allow for regular maintenance of the grounds.

Within cemeteries there may be specific sections with slightly different purposes. For example, there may be sections consecrated for meeting the needs of particular religious groups or an area specifically for children.

A church graveyard means that you are buried in consecrated ground associated with a church or group of churches.

"It seems like we have had most significant family events at that church. We went there as children, I was married there, and our children were christened there. I am so glad that we were able to bury Mum and Dad

there too because it is somewhere that we made some very happy memories together."

Flowers on a new grave

Most churchyards and cemeteries offer double graves and some offer graves for even greater numbers of people.

This could either involve the first person being buried at a deeper depth and the second person being placed on top or two people being buried beside each other.

Natural burial grounds are regarded as the most environmentally friendly choice for burial.

The graves are single depth, coffin, clothing and anything else placed in the grave must be natural and biodegradable, and embalming using formaldehyde is generally prohibited.

Any items placed on or around the grave at any time must also be biodegradable. Some natural burial grounds allow flowers, plants or trees to be planted on top of the grave but often these must be native to the area.

"Because our children were still so young she wanted to be buried in a place that they would feel comfortable visiting. She said that she felt that the natural burial ground was somewhere that we could come for a walk, or a picnic and she liked that it doesn't have any imposing headstones."

Woodland burial grounds are usually located in a woodland area and people are encouraged to plant trees near or on the grave of the person who has died.

Each woodland burial ground has its own set of principles and rules of how it will be run. Some woodland burial grounds follow the same principles as natural burial grounds whereas others do not place the same restrictions on coffin choice and grave markings.

It is extremely unusual to be able to buy or own a grave in a churchyard or cemetery. In most circumstances you can purchase exclusive rights of burial (often called grave deeds) within a burial ground.

This gives the right to be buried within that grave. The length of time for which this is valid from date of purchase varies between burial grounds.

For example, some allow you to purchase deeds for burial for 50 years but for other burial grounds this may be much longer.

In some locations deeds of burial can be purchased pre-emptively (effectively reserving the grave for use in the future), whereas in other locations the deeds can only be purchased at time of need. It's important to consider whose name will be placed on the grave deeds.

In some locations only the person named on the deeds may be placed in the grave or give permission for the grave to be used.

In that case, if someone purchases exclusive rights of burial and they die first then they will be unable to give permission for someone else in that family to use that grave afterwards. In some circumstances this has led to some challenges for family members further down the line.

Different burial locations offer different options regarding headstones and grave marking. It is likely that churchyards and cemeteries will allow headstones to be erected but each place will have its own set of rules and regulations which must be followed, and appropriate permissions will need to be granted.

Some woodland burial grounds allow headstones or plaques, whereas others do not, and a natural burial ground is unlikely to allow for a grave to be marked in this way.

Regardless of the way that the grave is externally marked, the managing agent is required to keep thorough and detailed records of which graves are in use, and who is buried there.

All the burial grounds have a different feel to them so if you are considering burial as an option then you might consider visiting the ones in your area to get a sense of them first.

"After visiting our local cemetery, we knew that it was the right place for Mum. It is peaceful and spacious and the views are magnificent. We reserved the plot beside her for Dad because he has always been clear that he would want to join her when his time comes."

Finally, burial at sea is an option at specified locations on the shores of the UK. Although possible, there are very specific requirements and the cost and complexity should not be underestimated.

Cremation

Flame cremation is a process of using heat to turn a body into ashes. Cremation occurs in a machine called a cremator which is usually located in a local authority or privately owned crematorium.

There are rules and regulations regarding cremation and specific paperwork which needs to be completed before cremation can take place.

There are restrictions around the materials which are allowed in a cremator and when being used for cremation coffin handles cannot be made of metal.

Almost all crematoria provide a dedicated space which can be used for the funeral service and each one is different in size, design and décor.

You are designated a timeslot for the service to take place (usually 30–50 minutes) and you need to enter the room, hold the service and leave the room during that time.

If this does not seem long enough, it is possible to book a double slot at the crematorium which costs a little more but gives you twice the time and removes much of the time pressure.

However, it is also possible to use a crematorium only for its ability to cremate, rather than as a place to have a service.

In that case, the words of committal might be spoken after the service elsewhere and the funeral director will bring the person who has died to the crematorium without family and friends being in attendance.

This often happens first thing in the morning and crematorium costs are generally reduced.

"Although we knew that she wanted to be cremated we thought that we would prefer

to have the service somewhere different and we decided to use the local village hall. We said our goodbyes at the end of the service and knew that the funeral director would be taking her to the crematorium the following morning."

In most crematoria there is a catafalque placed at the front of the service room.

This is where the coffin is usually resting during the funeral service. However, you may choose for the coffin to be placed on some trestles somewhere else in the room.

"We decided to put the coffin in the middle of the room because we wanted everyone to be able to gather around it in a circle. We had chosen a beautiful woollen coffin and it was soft and warm to touch."

In most cases you can choose for a curtain to close around the catafalque (between the coffin and the people who have gathered) but you can also ask that the curtain remains open as you leave the room.

Although less frequently available, some crematoria have catafalques that can lower or move away at the end of the service. Again, some people find this to be a helpful visual cue that the service has ended, whereas others do not.

If you choose to have the funeral service at the crematorium, I would suggest that you give some thought to what you would like to happen after the words of committal.

This can often be a very significant moment and you may find that you have strong views.

Would you prefer for the curtain to close after the words and for you to leave the room first and greet others as they leave?

Or would you like everyone else to be invited to leave the room first and for you to be left alone at the end of the service for a few minutes before joining people outside?

Would you like to leave the room first but approach the coffin as you leave, maybe leaving or taking a flower as you do so?

"Although we really wanted everyone to feel very welcome, we thought that a few minutes together as a family would be good for us. Everyone was asked to leave first and then we had a few private moments at the end. Afterwards many people told me that they thought that was really nice and could see themselves doing the same in future."

Some people would like to be able to witness the "charging of the coffin", which is when the coffin is placed into the cremator.

Some crematoria allow people to do so in person whereas others will only allow this to be witnessed using video.

If this is something that you would like to do, then your funeral director or staff at your local crematorium should be able to give you the support you need.

After a flame cremation has taken place, ashes are available for collection from the crematorium. There are a range of options available regarding what you can do with the ashes.

Direct cremation

Direct cremation is a process where the funeral director collects the person who has died and arranges for a cremation to take place.

With the exception of meeting with the funeral director to complete some paperwork, there are no funeral arrangements to be made and there is no funeral service.

The cremation is unattended and in a direct cremation there is usually no service at any other time either.

The ashes are made available for collection after the cremation and due to its simplicity, this is generally the cheapest way for a body to be buried or cremated.

Resomation (or Water Cremation)

Resomation, as an alternative to flame cremation, may be available in the future in the UK.

Resomation uses an alkaline solution and high pressure as an alternative to flames and heat in the cremation process.

It is currently available in the United States and it has been suggested that it is a more environmentally friendly alternative (and is therefore also known as green cremation).

As with flame cremation, ashes are available after resomation and the options regarding what you might like to do with the ashes are the same.

Please use the boxes below to write down a few of your thoughts.

Do you feel burial or cremation would be most appropriate? Is there any information that you need to make your final decision?

Has this chapter triggered any other thoughts?

Chapter 5

Locations and flow

Most people are familiar with the idea of a service taking place in a church or a crematorium. For many people this may be a meaningful place, particularly if the person who has died was an active member of a certain church or the family has a close connection to the local crematorium.

However, if you don't feel comfortable with either of these locations there are plenty of alternatives for you to choose from.

A church funeral

Unlike weddings, you don't need a specific licence to hold a funeral service and some funeral directors can offer a space for the service within their premises.

Furthermore, community centres, village halls, hotels, masonic lodges, conference centres, pubs, music venues and theatres are all possibilities, or you could choose to have the funeral in your own home.

A church funeral

Most venues are likely to do their best to accommodate a funeral whenever possible.

There are also a number of different ways to structure the timing and shape of the funeral. Both of these choices are influenced by a number of different factors.

Key considerations are whether the coffin will be present during the funeral service, and how many people you choose to invite at each stage. The options about how to time, and where to locate, different parts of the funeral are limitless and they are best illustrated by sharing some choices that people have kindly shared with me.

"Mum loved the church and had many friends there, so we had the service there and everyone was invited. It was important to Mum that she lay in church for her service and for people to be able to see her coffin there. After the service the family went straight to the crematorium. We wanted that part to be private because we found that time the hardest after Dad died twelve years ago. After the crematorium we joined everyone back at the local golf club for tea and sandwiches and we spent the afternoon sharing stories about a very fabulous lady."

"All of our family funerals have been at the crematorium and we like its simplicity and the fact that people don't have to travel around too much. We had the service there and then afterwards we went to the pub for a nice lunch and to spend time together."

"Dad had chosen a beautiful place to be buried and we decided that was also the best place to have the service. There were a few chairs available for people who were less able to stand but the rest of us stood at the graveside while the words were spoken. Someone had brought some portable speakers, so we could listen to some music and then after the service we all came back to my house for some tea and cake. It was a beautiful afternoon and I think he would have approved that we were out in nature, which is where he loved to be."

"We chose to have the service at the local community centre because it is a lovely spot and he chose it for his retirement party a few years before. After the service, the funeral director took him back to their place while we had lunch with our friends and

family. We met the funeral director again the following day and travelled to the graveside together. It worked well because it meant that we could spend the whole day with our friends and family and everyone was still invited to come to the burial if they wanted to."

"She had always said that she didn't want everyone travelling backward and forward for her funeral, so we decided to go to the crematorium first and invited some close friends and family to join us. After that very private and intimate committal service, we went for lunch together and then went to greet everyone as they arrived at the church for the longer memorial service. At the front of the church we had some beautiful flowers and lots of photos of Grandma for people to look at. We went across the road for the wake afterwards and it worked really well for us."

"I don't really like the crematorium, so we decided to have the service at a local hotel. It had a large function room (where they have lots of weddings) and we had the

funeral service there. We were able to personalise the room by putting photographs around the place and people sat around tables, rather than in rows. After the service, my husband left with the funeral director and they took him to the crematorium to be cremated. We stayed with our friends and family and listened to his favourite music and raised our glasses together."

"I really didn't want Dad's coffin to be present at his service. He was a very private man and he wouldn't have liked his coffin to be lying at the front of the room for everyone to see. We said our private goodbyes at the funeral home and then the funeral director arranged for him to be cremated. We knew when the cremation was happening, and we made sure that we were all together at my house. A few days later, we had a big service at Dad's rugby club and we brought his ashes because that felt right."

"He had told us time and time again that he didn't want a fuss and made us promise that we wouldn't hold a formal funeral service for him. At 97, many of his friends had died and those that were still alive would have found it hard to travel such a long way. So we respected his wishes and we asked the funeral director to arrange a direct cremation. Once we had his ashes, we scattered them with my mum's ashes and went for a very posh lunch."

"We decided that we wanted him to come home the night before the funeral. He rested in the living room and we brought him a cup of tea and sat around him chatting. I look back on that time really fondly and I am really glad that we had that opportunity to all be together."

These examples show the range of possibilities available and you may already have a preference as to what you feel would be most befitting of your circumstances.

Equally, you may be very clear what you don't feel comfortable with, or what would not be appropriate for the person who has died.

At this stage it is also worth considering what time of day would be best for you. Do people have far to travel or do some people need time to get ready in the morning?

Would you like the service to be later so people can come after a half day at work or would you prefer an early start? Would a Monday or Friday make most sense so that family and friends can stay for the weekend?

In most places it is possible for a funeral to take place during the weekend. It is likely that crematoria and burial grounds will have limited availability, but weekend funerals are slowly becoming more commonplace.

Funeral directors, crematoria and burial grounds are all likely to charge more for a weekend funeral.

These decisions may feel obvious, or you might be feeling overwhelmed at this point. If so, I suggest that you give yourself some time and speak to the other people involved. Once this decision has been made, many others will follow, and everything will start to feel clearer.

With locations and preferred timings decided upon, the funeral director (or you if you prefer) will be able to start liaising with all the relevant places and people to make the necessary reservations.

Once you can start sharing the date, time and location with people then that can often feel like a big relief. Furthermore, it is often the first step in gaining some insight into the number of people who are likely to be able to attend.

Please use the boxes below to write down a few of your thoughts.

What are your current thoughts about the best service and committal locations?

Do you have any preferences about the timing and order of events?

Is there any more information that you need?

Has this chapter triggered any other thoughts?

Chapter 6

People, words and involvement

Funerals in three parts

When considering a funeral, you might find it helpful to think of it in three overlapping sections and the next three chapters consider each of these in turn. At each different stage, you can be involved and create meaning if you want to.

However, you may feel that one aspect is more important to you personally and focus most of your time on that instead.

Firstly, there are the words that will be spoken during a service. These may be planned or informal and may be delivered by one person, or by many different people.

Secondly, there is everything else on the day of the funeral. This includes the music and many visual and tangible things such as flowers, cars and the coffin.

Thirdly, there is the time between the person dying and the funeral itself. This is the time during which funeral arrangements are being made and many tasks are being completed, some of which may be very helpful to you and support you to find a growing acceptance of what has happened.

The officiant or celebrant

Although a funeral director will help you to make most of the funeral arrangements, it is usually someone else who will support you to create and conduct the service. There are four main groups of people who perform this role and they include religious leaders, civil celebrants, humanist celebrants and friends or family.

Your reflections prompted by previous chapters are likely to help you decide which type of officiant would be most appropriate.

Religious leaders may be affiliated with a church, synagogue or other place of worship and if you have chosen to have a service in one of these locations, then the choice of officiant may be the person associated with that place.

However, if you have a close relationship with someone suitably qualified, who is not immediately connected to a specific place of worship, they may be given permission to conduct the service there.

Many religious leaders are also happy to conduct a service outside their religious location (for example at the crematorium or a function room) so it is possible to have a religious service without being in a church.

"Mum hadn't been to church for some time, so she didn't know the current minister. We

asked the retired minister whether he would be able to conduct the service for her and we are so glad that he could. It meant a lot to us that Mum's service was done by someone who knew her personally."

Civil celebrants are usually specifically trained to deliver a number of ceremonies including funeral services, and this is often their full-time profession.

They will help you to decide the best structure and content for the service and will include as much or as little religious content as you like.

Either the celebrant can deliver all the words on the day of the funeral, or friends and family can be involved as much as you would like them to be.

Humanist celebrants deliver non-religious, secular funeral services and they believe that human needs and values are more important than religious beliefs. They will also help you to decide the best structure and content for the service but will not be willing to deliver any religious words themselves, as this is contrary to their personal beliefs.

Some humanist celebrants will step aside and allow someone else to deliver a prayer during the service (because they recognise that people present may have different needs) but if you would like any more than this then a humanist service might not be the most appropriate choice.

"We didn't feel that religion had a part to play at Dad's funeral and we wanted the service to be all about him. He went to a friend's funeral a few months previously and commented that he really liked the service. We found out which humanist celebrant had delivered that service and asked her to help us with Dad's funeral because it felt like he had chosen her himself."

Finally, friends and family could conduct the service themselves. There are no rules about who must conduct a funeral and there are many written and online resources available to give guidance.

Some families choose to create a structured service, whereas others may facilitate a more informal gathering and sharing of memories.

"We didn't like the idea of telling someone about Mum and then have them repeat that information back to us. Luckily, my brother is a lecturer and felt that he would like to lead the service for us all. We drew on our collective funeral experiences, looked at some orders of service sheets we had between us and put something together ourselves."

Once you have decided which type of officiant would be most appropriate for your circumstances your funeral director should be able to recommend a few local people to you.

Alternatively, you may already have someone in mind, or seek a recommendation from people you know. You may also choose to search online for people in your area.

Different celebrants are likely to have their own unique styles and personalities. They are responsible for supporting you to create a service and will then deliver some or all of the words on the day. It is important that you feel confident that you will be able to rapidly establish a constructive rapport with them and that you can trust them to competently fulfil your wishes.

I would suggest that you speak to them on the telephone initially to make sure that you feel able to make the right connection with them, before making the final decision to engage their services.

Choosing the words

Although there are no rules about what should be included in a service, many services include an introduction, poems or readings, a tribute or eulogy, prayers and words of committal.

The individual who is conducting the service should guide you in these choices but there are some questions that might help you to start to gather your thoughts in the meantime.

Would you like to acknowledge the loss, celebrate the life, or a mixture of the two? Would you like to include reference to your beliefs about what happens after life?

Would you like a traditional eulogy, or would you prefer to include a compilation of memories and stories? Is there anyone who might like to stand and speak?

In a religious service, the words of committal are likely to be guided by scripture and beliefs about the afterlife.

In an otherwise secular service, religious words of committal may still feel most appropriate but there are also many humanist, or non-religious alternatives.

Again, there is much written and online guidance and your officiant will give you options based on the preferences you have expressed.

"He was a very factual man and it was important that the words of committal reflected that. He believed that when you are gone, you are gone. Although I believe in something quite different, I felt that it was important that the words were true to his belief."

If you have chosen to have the service at the crematorium you need to remember that you have a designated time slot there and that you need to ensure that you stay within that time.

It is possible to book a double slot at the crematorium and you might want to consider this, rather than excluding content that you would like to be included.

"We knew quite early on that there were going to be a quite a few people who might like to stand up and say something. Rather than start restricting the number of people or being strict with them about how long they could have, we booked a double service slot and that gave us one less thing to worry about."

It is important for me to mention that you do not have to include any prepared words at the funeral at all. Many people find the presence of a structure reassuring and appropriate, but others prefer to invite people to contribute freely if they want to, or to simply sit and listen to music.

"My brother and I didn't feel that it was a time for words. The two of us gathered at the graveside and just spent some time there. When we felt ready, we asked the funeral director to lower Mum's coffin. It was minimal, simple and right for us."

Involvement and participation

There are many opportunities for people to be involved and participate during the arrangement process and at the funeral itself.

Some people have told me that the opportunity to be involved has been helpful to them as it has given them positive memories and allowed them to express themselves and acknowledge the significance of the loss they have experienced.

Participation can be done publicly (like a eulogy) or privately (like choosing the photographs for the written service sheet). It can also be done as an individual, or a group (like pallbearing).

However, for others this might not be helpful at all. By exploring what is possible, you might recognise opportunities that are right for you, or be able to make suggestions to others, but please don't feel any pressure to take part in anything that you don't want to.

Some examples of how people have chosen to be involved in the service are best illustrated in the following quotes.

"It was really important to me that I write and deliver my Dad's eulogy. He did a fabulous speech at my wedding and at his funeral, it was my turn to return the favour. I think I did him proud."

"My brothers and I didn't want to stand up and speak but we wanted the words at the funeral to be ours, not written by someone who didn't know Mum. So, we wrote the tribute and reflections and they were read by the celebrant on the day. We were glad we did it like that because we could really listen to what was being said rather than spend the whole day worrying about whether we would be in a fit state to deliver them ourselves."

"She was so very important to many, many people and we wanted to capture that during the service. So, we invited everyone we knew to share a memory or message by email and then we collated them into groups and themes. There were a few things that came up again and again, so it worked well, and I liked that we managed to include many, many people."

"I really wanted to say something but had been feeling very emotional so decided to read out a poem, rather than speak my own words. I chose a hopeful, uplifting poem

because I thought I could manage that. Although my voice cracked at the very end, I am really glad that I did it."

"I chose to read an old proverb that I think summed Mum up perfectly. I was worried that I might not want to stand up on the day, so the celebrant and I agreed that she would have a copy and I could just nod to her and she would read it instead of me. Just knowing that was a possibility seemed to make me feel less anxious."

"During one of the pieces of music, my brothers and sisters and I came up and put a white rose on Mum's coffin. She loved roses and it felt right that we each give her one at the service."

"There weren't enough family and friends to carry the coffin alone, so my brother and husband carried Mum in with the help of two people that the funeral director arranged. I can't imagine that it was an easy thing to do but I know that was something important to my brother."

"All the ladies were given a red rose as they left the church and were then invited to place the rose into the grave after the burial had taken place. Roses were her favourite and I think it gave people the chance to be involved."

Family and friends placing lavender in the grave at a burial service

There are also many ways that people can be included during the time after the service, the refreshments or after-funeral wake.

"Mum's friends are brilliant at arranging flowers, so we asked them if they would help to make the room look nice and bright

for afterwards. They got together and made ten lovely table arrangements with Mum's favourite flowers in glass jars and I'm really glad that I asked them."

"Dad's best friend is great at speaking at events, so we asked him if he would propose a toast when we arrived at the hotel. I could tell that he felt that it was a great honour and it was very nice to see so many friends and family raise a glass to my dad."

"Rather than have a book of condolence for guests to write in, we put out pieces of card for people to write a message on. The four grandchildren decorated a cardboard post box, which we had bought from a local craft shop, and everyone posted their messages in there. The children were pleased to be asked to do such an important job and the green and gold sparkly post box was really something."

"We asked everyone to bring a photograph of Dad to the service and they added them to a collage board during refreshments. Not everyone brought one but the ones that we

*did receive are very precious to us and we
have put them in a book for Mum."*

Children and funerals

To some people it is obvious whether the
children in their lives should or should not
be involved in the funeral arrangements
and funeral itself.

However, to many others this decision
seems difficult and there might be strong
opposing views within the same family (and
between parents).

Once people have decided whether children
should or should not be included, then
working out how to do so in the best
possible way can also cause anxiety.

As with all funeral decisions, the most
appropriate approach will depend on the
circumstances and the people involved.

In my experience, people worry that
involving children will cause them to be
upset and that it might lead them to realise

that people die and to start to ruminate about that.

Some people have also expressed concern that if a child gets upset or doesn't behave impeccably, this might not be acceptable to others present.

Parents may not want to be worrying about their children on the day, to enable them to focus on the funeral themselves.

Although these worries are entirely valid, there are also strong counterarguments to each of these concerns.

Children are likely to experience a significant bereavement before they reach adulthood so it is unlikely that you can protect them from the reality that people die.

In fact, supporting them to accept this may well be very helpful to them developing the resilience that will help them to cope with the challenges that they will inevitably face.

Most people are very tolerant to children expressing emotion (or getting a bit distracted) at funerals and in my experience, children usually understand the importance of the event and behave in a befitting manner.

I have seen many children give a very well-timed hug or pass over a much-needed tissue. Seeing the adults in their life cry might help them to be better able to understand and express their own emotions.

If you are unsure about what to do for the best, then I would suggest introducing the idea very gently and seeing how they respond.

You could tell them a little about the arrangements so far, or there are many brilliant books written specifically for children, which you could read with them.

Asking them if they have any questions might help to elicit what their thoughts are. Sometimes suggesting that they write down any worries or draw a picture to show how they are feeling might help.

You could ask them if they want you to tell them what will be happening at the funeral and then give them the information they are looking for.

If they are very open to talking and seem interested and engaged, then the conversation may evolve and give you a good idea about whether they would like to be involved or not.

In contrast, if they really don't want to talk about it and deflect the questions then you could tell them that you are ready to talk about it if they want to, but you might not want to push the subject any further.

Without the opportunity to ask questions, and be given accurate information, children may well fill in the blanks themselves.

It is very unlikely that they will be oblivious to what has happened, and their imagination may well draw conclusions which are more frightening than reality.

Inviting children to write a note to the person who has died, draw a picture for them or help you to choose flowers or photographs might be gentle ways to involve them in the funeral.

Their reaction might also help you to gauge whether their attendance would be helpful and right for them.

Writing notes

Children decorating letters to accompany the coffin

Although there are many ways to include children, and I would strongly encourage you to consider doing so, you might not feel able to.

If that is the case, then that is okay. If including them at the time of the funeral seems too challenging, then you might consider including them in a post-funeral commemorative informal event instead.

These are considered in a chapter later in this book.

Please use the boxes below to write down a few of your thoughts.

What type of officiant do you feel would be most appropriate?

Do you have any current thoughts about people being involved in the funeral service?

Do you have any current thoughts about what you might like to include?

Would you, or anyone else like to deliver some or all of the service?

Are there any children that you would like to consider as part of these arrangements, or the funeral itself?

Chapter 7

Everything but the words

There is no right way

There are many options about what you can include in and around a funeral but other than the bare minimum, very little is necessary.

This chapter will give you an overview of the different possibilities and hopefully it will give you a few ideas about what you would like.

The range of options is enormous, and it is overwhelming to be presented with every possible choice, so a funeral director is likely to help you to expand on your existing ideas by making a few related suggestions for you to consider, rather than presenting you with every possibility.

I would suggest that you give some consideration to what other people who are important to you think, but don't be unduly concerned about what you "should" choose.

If you listen to what your gut instinct is telling you is right, then that can be more helpful than trying to guess what other people might think.

Funerals can be very expensive and although some costs are unavoidable, I would encourage you to try to only spend money on things that you value whenever possible.

When you are weighing up the various possibilities and making your choices, it is important to know the prices associated with the different options.

Only when you know the price can you determine whether you are spending money on the things that are important to you.

Newspaper notifications

Most local, regional and national newspapers have a dedicated section in their written and online publications for death notifications.

There is often a set format that the paper uses but you are usually very welcome to deviate from this template if you prefer.

The price largely depends on the length of the notification, the distribution of the paper and where you are located.

Some people place a notification because they feel that it is important and because they would like to keep a copy of the relevant papers.

Others place a notice in a paper because they want to make sure that they have done everything they possibly can to notify everyone in a certain location that the death has occurred and what the funeral arrangements are.

Many people now use other methods to communicate that someone has died, and to provide people with details of the funeral.

Email, social media channels and dedicated memorial websites are often used and less commonly people choose to send notification cards.

It is not uncommon for people to announce that someone has died using their social media profiles.

Furthermore, there are settings on platforms such as Facebook that allow accounts to be memorialised, enabling friends and family to make contributions by sharing photographs and memories.

Coffin

Choosing can be difficult, as it is a powerful visual symbol of funerals. Whereas some people feel very indifferent about this choice, others have strong views about what they would or would not like.

Most people are familiar with wooden coffins and they are available in a variety of shapes, designs and colours.

Wooden coffins are usually made from either laminated or solid wood and the price is influenced by the amount and type of wood.

They range from the very simple to the very ornate and can be in a lighter shade (such as natural oak or pine) or a darker tone like mahogany.

The shape that most people are familiar with is either a silhouette shape (wider at the shoulders and tapered at the feet and head), or the rectangular shape of a casket.

More contemporary designs are also available, such as those with rounded ends or curved tops.

Handles are usually made from brass, plastic or wood. When used for cremation, the handles can't be made of brass and plastic (brass coloured) handles are used instead.

If you would preference a wooden coffin for a natural burial then an unvarnished wooden coffin, with wooden handles and made from sustainably sourced wood, is probably the best choice. The same applies if you would simply like to minimise the environmental impact of your wooden coffin choice.

"We really liked the natural burial ground but were also very sure that Dad would have wanted a wooden coffin. When we realised that we could use certain wooden coffins at the burial ground, it felt like the perfect choice for us."

Unvarnished wooden coffin with wooden handles and a dried hydrangea wreath

There are various alternatives to wood available. Wicker coffins, woollen coffins and cardboard coffins are being chosen more and more frequently and are also regarded as more environmentally friendly.

Again, there are a variety of shapes and styles available in wicker coffins and they can be woven from a range of materials such as banana, willow and bamboo.

Wicker with sunflowers

"She always loved crafting and knitting and enjoyed the textures of different materials. When we saw a photo of the woollen coffin, we knew that she would have appreciated that. We felt that everyone at the funeral agreed that it was the right choice for her."

A woollen coffin

There is also a huge range of cardboard, MDF and wood veneer coffins with different images printed on them (for example of flowers, sports and beautiful scenes) and it is also possible to send your own images or designs to be used to decorate the coffin.

Furthermore, most coffin materials can be painted in any colour that you choose, and plain cardboard coffins are great to use as a blank canvas to decorate.

"The celebrant suggested that we could invite people to write a message on the coffin during the service. Initially we weren't

sure but then when we spoke to a few of our friends about it, we realised that it could be something quite special. We chose a white cardboard coffin so that people could easily write on it."

Finally, you don't have to use a coffin at all. Cotton, bamboo and felt shrouds are also available and provide yet another alternative.

I would suggest having a look at one of each type of coffin (and their prices) and when you have decided which you prefer then you could look at more choices within that category.

Flowers

Flowers can be an important part of the funeral for many people. Flowers can be placed on the coffin, used to decorate the service room (for example on pedestals or as pew ends) and specific shapes and designs can be a means of personalisation.

In the past, many people would bring flowers to the funeral to show their respect and to acknowledge the importance of the event. Increasingly, families are asking that people make donations to charity in memory of the person who has died "in lieu of flowers".

A few simple blooms or a huge display can both look stunning and I would suggest you ask yourself a few questions before making your final decision about flowers.

Are flowers important to the person who has died? Are they important to anyone else who is attending?

Do you associate the person who has died with a particular flower? Would you prefer something neat or something a little more natural looking?

Is there a shape that you like; for example, a cross, heart, wreath or double ended spray?

A basket of flowers

You will be able to find inspiration from your local florist, funeral director or online and a little research will hopefully result in a flower arrangement that you are happy with. Floral letters, aeroplanes, guitars, football shirts and many, many more can be created by very talented florists and as an interesting variation for an avid gardener, vegetables could even be included.

If you would like to include a written message or tribute with the flower arrangement then your funeral director or florist will be able to give you a flower card, or you can dictate a message for them to write on your behalf.

A flower and vegetable arrangement

"She loved wildflowers and we all prefer more natural, less tidy flower arrangements. We asked the florist to make an arrangement that looked like flowers growing naturally in a country garden with grasses included. Mum would have loved it."

"She really loved her doll's house, so we asked the florist to surround it with beautiful flowers made to look like a cottage garden. We included sweet peas because she would always pick bunches of them from the garden when no one was looking."

Some people choose to arrange the flowers themselves, maybe including flowers from their garden, or choose for a flower garland to be woven into a wicker coffin.

Others prefer to use potted plants such as chillies or strawberries, or bunches of dried rosemary or lavender can be used instead.

Permanent decorative wreaths or artificial flowers can also be good alternatives for people who don't want to use the fresh alternative.

"He didn't particularly like flowers and always said that cut flowers were a complete waste of money. So, we asked the florist to make a small arrangement of moss and some simple flowers with his walking boots in the middle. It was something a little different and everyone commented on how appropriate it was for him."

Walking boots

You might like to include some personal items within the flower display. Plants can be placed in well-worn walking boots, a trowel and terracotta pot could take centre stage in the display, or a pot of paint and paintbrush might feature.

It is possible to attach a flower and foliage garland or posies to the side of a wicker coffin so that it is surrounded by flowers. Some people choose to be involved in creating and attaching the garland (usually with the help of a florist) to the coffin.

Wicker coffin, decorated by friends and family using foraged flowers and foliage

If posies have been used, then these can be detached from the coffin immediately before the physical committal and can be given to people to take away.

Wicker with garland

"We chose a wicker coffin with one flower arrangement on top and some posies around the edges. The four posies were

given to her best friends afterwards and I believe they have dried them and now have them hanging up at home."

Wicker with posies

The flowers could stay with the coffin after the committal, or you might like to take the flowers for everyone to enjoy during refreshments afterwards.

Some people choose to leave the flowers on the grave, or if cremation has been chosen, leave them on the grave of another family member or close friend.

Flowers or foliage can also be used to dress a grave. Placed around the surround and within the grave, they can soften the image of the grave slightly and the addition of favourite flowers, or items from the garden can be meaningful for those attending.

As an alternative to placing soil into a grave after the committal, flowers, rosemary or lavender can be used.

A dressed grave

Other coffin toppers

Other items can be placed on top of the coffin, either instead of flowers, or in addition to them.

Flags could be placed on the coffin, particularly if they acknowledge the importance of a place or event.

Medals, caps, a university tie, a model aeroplane or train or a copy of a favourite magazine or newspaper can be a subtle means of personalisation. Equally, a favourite photograph can be placed on, or in front of, the coffin, or some personalised bunting draped over the top.

"He made model planes his whole life and the flying club was hugely important to him. We chose a plane that he built to be placed on the top of his coffin during the service and having it there made everything a little easier for us."

Although not strictly "coffin toppers", larger items can be placed beside or in front of the coffin. For example, a knitting basket full of wool, a bicycle, guitar or cherished painting or creation may feel like a fitting addition.

Coffin bunting

Cars and travel

It is not a legal requirement to use a hearse and you can use any vehicle which is large enough, for example an estate car.

However, the majority of people find that a hearse is the most appropriate choice for them. Most people are familiar with a traditional hearse and limousine but there are many alternatives.

Different makes and colours are possible and vintage cars, motorbikes, Volkswagen campervans and lorry hearse conversions are all available.

Horse-drawn carriages, in a variety of colours, can be chosen and there is even a London bus hearse.

"He was a very traditional gentleman and always tipped his hat when a funeral cortege passed by on the street. A traditional hearse and limousine were definitely the right choice for him."

Electric hearses are a silent, environmentally friendly alternative and they may also appeal to people who don't identify with the size and grandeur of their traditional counterpart.

If there is a vehicle which resonates with you as befitting of the person who has died, then it is worth exploring whether it is a possibility. I know of people who have arrived at their funeral in a helicopter!

"She always liked things that were a little different and said on a number of occasions that she found large hearses a little imposing. We chose a smaller, electric hearse because it was more understated, and I think she would have liked that we chose something relatively rare."

Nissan Leaf electric hearse with a wicker coffin

Some people find limousines convenient and an important inclusion in the funeral cortege. Others would rather travel in their own vehicles or ask relatives and friends to drive them. Both choices work perfectly well, and it boils down to personal preference.

There may be some special local places that you would like the person who has died to drive past, or stop outside, on their journey to the service or committal.

For example, for some it is important to pass the family home, a church where they were married, a favourite pub, or significant place of work.

Again, this is by no means compulsory, but knowing that it is possible is the first step in establishing whether it feels helpful to you or not.

People have different opinions about whether they would like to travel with the hearse on the day of the funeral.

For some, travelling as part of the cortege (whether in a limousine or not) is an important part of the funeral whereas others would rather be at the crematorium, church or other location to meet guests and the hearse as it arrives.

When travelling with the hearse, you could leave from the funeral director's premises together, or you might prefer to be collected on the way (maybe at a family member's house).

"We wanted Dad to come back past his home on the way to the crematorium, so we chose for the hearse and limousine to pick us up there. We gathered together in the house and all felt very emotional when we saw him approaching. The journey to the crematorium gave us time to gather our thoughts and when we arrived we felt ready to go into the funeral and see people."

Funeral directors will usually offer to walk in front of the hearse at various points on the journey. Typically, this will be on arrival and leaving the house and when approaching the service or committal venues.

This is called "paging" and some people feel that it is a very respectful and reverential

117

way to depart and arrive. For others, it is a ritual that they would rather avoid, so do make sure that you express your preferences to your funeral director.

On arrival, the coffin will need to be taken from the hearse into the service room, or to the graveside.

This can be done by professionals (i.e. people organised by the funeral director), family and friends (male and female), or a combination of the two.

Some funeral directors are more encouraging of family participation than others but if this is important to you then there should be a way for that to be possible.

You may wish to be present or take part in placing the coffin into the hearse; there is no reason for this not to be allowed.

"It was very important to my brother and my sons that they were able to carry Mum's coffin. I was worried that it would be too much pressure for them, but they were

adamant that was something they wanted to do. The image of them coming towards me carrying Mum was very, very moving and will stay with me forever."

"I wanted to make sure that she had one of us with her for every part of the journey. My husband helped to put her into the hearse and then we both travelled in the hearse with her. At the cemetery, four of us carried her to her grave and lowered her in. It is the hardest thing that I have ever done but I am so glad that we found it in ourselves to do it for her."

Depending on your coffin choice and the route you need to take, there are three possible ways for the coffin to be transported from the hearse into the service location.

Firstly, the coffin could be lifted onto the shoulders of four to six people and carried. Six people are better when the coffin is heavy, but with that many people it is important to make sure that someone communicates which leg people are to start walking with to avoid bearers' feet bumping into each other en route.

Shouldering the coffin is more physically demanding but to some people it is very meaningful and important to them to be able to participate.

As an alternative to carrying the coffin on shoulders, some coffins enable four or six people to carry it by holding on to the handles on the sides.

In that case, the coffin doesn't have to be lifted onto the shoulders and it means the young, or physically less able can take part (especially if they are positioned towards the middle of the coffin).

This is only possible if the handles are load-bearing (like many wicker, woollen or cardboard coffins), rather than merely decorative (as with many plastic handles on wooden coffins).

"We chose a wicker coffin and wanted to carry it as a family. At the burial ground there was quite a distance to the grave, so

we decided to hold the coffin by the six handles and then people could swap if their hands got too tired. It meant that my elderly dad and my young son could also take a short turn and although some people would have found this a little informal, it worked really well for us."

Finally, the coffin could be placed on a trolley and then pushed to the necessary place.

This might not be possible if the ground is very uneven or there are many steps to navigate and your funeral director should be able to guide you about which options are possible in your case.

Some people prefer for the coffin to already be present when they arrive. You may still have a clear preference about the choice of vehicle for the person who has died, or want to travel in limousines yourselves, but just not want to personally see the movement of the coffin.

As with many funeral choices, I would suggest that you give yourself the time you need to decide what is best for you, and then stay true to those preferences.

Written service sheets

Once the content and flow of the service have been agreed, this can be used to create a written service sheet or "Order of Service".

This can be handed to guests as they arrive, or left on chairs or pews for people to pick up as they take their seats.

You do not have to have a written service sheet, but they can be helpful if you would like people to sing hymns or join in certain prayers which they may not be familiar with.

In churches and many crematoria, hymn books are available but outside of these locations it is unlikely that they will be present.

Some people also recognise that friends, family and guests may wish to keep the booklet in memory of the funeral and the person who has died.

"Having a written service booklet was important to me because I know that many people keep them. I also wanted to be able to send them to people who weren't able to come to the funeral so that they also felt included."

Some people also choose to include the words of a poem or reading that they regard as especially poignant and add details of the chosen charity for donations. You can also include information about refreshments, if you have arranged to have any after the service.

Although A5 booklets are the most well-known choice, you could also choose a postcard or a bookmark size instead.

The written sheet can be very simple, it could include a photograph of the person who has died, or it might include many photographs and become more like a story book of someone's life.

It can be as simple or elaborate as you would like, and you might like to delegate its design to a creative friend or relative.

"I spent many hours looking at photographs and then putting a service sheet together. The process seemed really cathartic and it felt like an act of love to create something special and memorable."

Photographs, slide shows and videos

Some people choose not to include any photographs as part of the funeral but for people who would like to, there are several different ways that it can be done.

A framed photograph could be included on, or in front of, the coffin during the service, or positioned on the front of the written service sheet.

More than one photograph can be included in the written service sheet, and this might be an opportunity to include photographs of the person who has died at different times in their life, doing things they enjoyed or with other significant people included.

It is also possible to create a photo collage on a pin board or pegged to an old picture frame with string strung across it. This could be placed at the front of the service room, or on a table during refreshments afterwards.

"We had so many fabulous photographs of her that there was no way that we were going to be able to narrow it down to one or two. We spent a really nice afternoon making a picture collage and the photos seemed to trigger different memories which we thought we had forgotten."

Many people now hold most of their photographs digitally and that creates the opportunity to have a photograph slide show.

Again, this could be shown during the service (maybe while listening to a reflective piece of music) or during refreshments afterwards. Videos can also be included in the service and could be of the person who has died, or of events and places that are of importance.

As I mentioned previously, some people don't want to use photographs (or may have been given specific instructions by the person who has died not to do so) and other people have so many photos that they would like to use that they don't know where to start.

There is no right or wrong way and you are the best person to decide what is the best approach for you.

Although still relatively uncommon, it is possible to live-stream the funeral to people who cannot attend (but have access to the internet).

It is also possible to hire a professional photographer or videographer to record the service, or to ask someone you know to try to capture some key parts for you.

This is not a choice that would appeal to everybody but is worth considering if you think that a lasting image of some aspects of the funeral might be helpful to you.

Donations

You may wish to name a charity for people to make donations to in memory of the person who has died. Again, this is not compulsory, and some people decide that they don't want to do that.

However, if this is something that you would like to do then you might like to have a donations box present at the end of the service, or you may prefer for donations to be made online instead.

The choice of charity is likely to be influenced by the interests and beliefs of the person who has died, the cause of their death and whether there are any charities that they actively supported.

To some people the choice of charity is immediately obvious, whereas to others this decision is a little harder.

It is an opportunity to support a charity close to their heart, or to acknowledge the support that they received from certain organisations towards the end of their life (for example a local hospice). It is also an opportunity to contribute to raising awareness about an illness they may have had, or to support research into causes and treatment of their condition.

You may wish to choose two charities and spread any donations between them.

There are several ways of collecting donations online and this may be worth considering if you are planning any ongoing fundraising activities.

For example, if you would like to engage in any events at a later stage to raise money for the same charity then the fundraising page could remain open beyond the funeral date.

"My son said that he wanted to do a bike ride to raise money in memory of his brother. I had heard that some people find that things like that can help with their grief, so I wanted to encourage him as much as I could. We opened a donations page for the funeral and then he shared it again when he was getting ready to do his bike ride."

In addition to well-known fundraising websites, there are also specific memorial websites which allow you to share memories and manage donations at the same time.

Most fundraising websites take a proportion of the donations as their administration fees, so it is worth checking the terms carefully before you make your final choice.

Dress code

Some people feel that it is most appropriate to wear black to a funeral, some people would prefer people to wear anything but black, and there are many possibilities in between.

If you have a preference about what people will wear, then the newspaper or online notifications are a good opportunity to communicate that to people who will be attending.

Did the person who has died give you any instructions about what people should wear? Would you like people to wear something representing a favourite colour?

Do you want people to come in whatever they feel comfortable in? Would you like people to adhere to a theme or is it not something that you feel is important?

"The only thing that we knew is that she didn't want people to wear black. It was important to us that we managed to fulfil her one request, so we chose a few people and made them responsible for making sure that everyone knew."

People attending funerals are often worried about doing something "wrong", or to cause offence to the family of the person who has died. In my experience, people like to be given clear instructions and are generally very happy to oblige.

In the absence of an instruction, people generally make a sensible judgement themselves about what is most fitting given the person and location.

Record of attendance

Some people would like to have a record of who attended the funeral and there are several ways that can be achieved.

Cards can be placed on seats or handed to people as they arrive for them to complete. These could also request contact details, so that family members can send a thank you card after the funeral has taken place.

Rather than just recording who has attended, some families ask guests to write a memory or tell them something that they don't already know about the person who has died.

This could be written in a book or on a card to be placed in a basket or special post box, or on a tag to be tied to the branches of a memory tree. Words can be written on pebbles to be placed in a jar or people can be asked to add their ink fingerprint to the outline of a tree drawn on canvas.

Tags on a memory tree

"We asked people to share a memory on a card. During refreshments, when we looked around the room we could see people sitting at different tables writing their messages.

They seemed to be doing it with great care and that meant a lot to us."

After the funeral, these messages can be collated and placed in a book or box to be read when the time feels right.

As with many possibilities mentioned in this chapter, you may either identify with the suggestion, or might not feel that they are right for you.

The funeral aims to reflect the person who has died and be helpful to you, so please don't feel any pressure to include anything that doesn't resonate with you.

Entering and exiting

I would suggest giving a little thought to the beginning and end of the service.

At the start of the service, you may want to follow the coffin into the room, with all the other guests following you. In contrast you may prefer for everyone to be seated first and for the coffin then to enter. The former is more common in the crematorium and the latter in a church, but either is possible in both places.

If you have chosen for the coffin to arrive at the service location before the guests have started to congregate, then it is likely that people will start to take their seats as they arrive. In this case you may choose to do the same, or you might want to walk in with the officiant as the service starts.

"We wanted to greet people as they arrived, rather than walking in to a sea of faces. We arrived an hour early and had the chance to speak to most people as they came in. It made for a lovely atmosphere and we were really aware of how many people were there to support us."

It is usual for family and close friends to take the seats closest to the front of the service room.

If everyone is entering together and they are positioned towards the front of the group, then they will naturally end up at the front seats.

If you have a preference about who you will be sitting next to, or where other specific individuals will be seated, then it might be worth making sure that the relevant people know what you would like in advance.

If guests are taking their seats as they arrive then it is wise to have the correct number of seats reserved at the front. Once you know how many people need a reserved seat, then the funeral director or verger should take care of the rest.

At the end of the service there are several options. You may wish to leave first (approaching the coffin if you want to) or invite other guests to leave before you, leaving you alone for a few minutes at the end.

Some people would like to greet and shake hands with guests as they leave the service room, whereas others would rather do that at another time. If you have arranged to be at the service location early, then you might have already greeted many people as they arrived.

Alternatively, you could choose to wait to speak to people during refreshments rather than immediately after the service and committal.

Once you have decided what you feel would work best for you, your family and friends, then the funeral director and officiant should take care of gently directing guests as required.

The officiant will give clear direction at the end of the service as to who should leave first and where people should congregate afterwards.

Items to take away

As with other significant events (like weddings), some people like to give guests a gift, a keepsake to take away to remember the day or in memory of the person who has died.

This may be a candle, a book token or a packet of forget-me-not seeds to be sown in remembrance. It may be that there is a more specific item which is an obvious choice given the person who has died.

If they loved a certain flower, then a flower bulb to be planted in their memory might feel meaningful. If there was a sweet or chocolate that they were known to love, then one could be offered to each of the guests as they leave the service.

"She was always eating chocolate so we thought that it would be nice for everyone to be given a chocolate on the way out. I hope that when people eat that same chocolate from now on they will remember her infectious laugh and that it makes them smile."

As with many of these options, they might give you an idea which you find helpful but if they don't, then that is okay. No-one is expecting to be given anything and there is no pressure to do so.

Please use the boxes below to write down a few of your thoughts.

Newspaper notification?

Coffin?

Cars, travel and carrying the coffin?

Flowers and other coffin toppers?

Dress code and items to take away?

Written service sheets and records of attendance?

Photographs and audio-visual technology?

Entering and exiting the service?

Any other thoughts prompted by this chapter

Chapter 8

Time before the funeral

Meaningful tasks

The time between someone dying and their funeral taking place is the time in which many of the arrangements are being made, and it can be a very busy and overwhelming time.

Although much of the focus will be on the day of the funeral, it is also worth considering whether there are any tasks or activities that you might find meaningful and helpful during this period.

For example, some people find the time with family and friends choosing photographs for the written service document to be very helpful and positive.

Similarly, sharing memories and stories while deciding which words might be included in the service can be a powerful and cathartic experience for some. Visiting the florist and choosing beautiful flowers can also be a creative and meaningful time.

Family members gather to create a flower arrangement

Some find the task of choosing clothes for the person who has died to be very meaningful and describe it as a very important job to be executed with care and love.

Others find the process of writing a card or letter to be placed in the coffin to be personal and helpful. You may not feel that any of these activities would help you and that is okay.

However, knowing what others have found helpful might prompt you to recognise something you may not otherwise have thought of.

"I spent quite some time with the people from the venue where we were going to have refreshments. Choosing a menu that she would have been happy with and deciding how the room might be laid out seemed important. I see now that I was coping by keeping myself busy and focussing on the part of the arrangements that I felt most familiar with."

Caring for the person who has died

The funeral director will collect the person who has died and bring them into their care.

They will care for their body and guide you about how this can be done. Some funeral directors are likely to be more forthcoming about discussing this than others.

Thinking about how the person who has died will be looked after can be very difficult for some people and therefore I will not go into any detail in this book.

Suffice to say that there are a number of different options and I find it helpful to think of it as a continuum of personal care.

From washing and dressing to more specialist methods, funeral directors have several different ways that they can care for someone.

There are some religions and cultures where specific care rituals should be honoured, and if that is the case then you are likely to be offered support from peers within that community, or you may wish to choose a funeral director who is also from the same religion or culture.

As our cultures become more diverse, some people may choose to adhere to certain rituals that they find meaningful and decline to engage in others that they find less so.

Once you have decided what is right for your circumstances then this might be something that you would like to discuss with your funeral director in more detail.

You may also want to be involved in some aspects of this personal care. For many people this feels too difficult and not something that they would find helpful, but for other people it is something that they would like to take an active part in.

Again, this is something that you could discuss with your funeral director and is completely down to your own personal choice.

"I had cared for him for many years before he died, and it suddenly felt important for me to be able to do it one last time. It was difficult, but I am so glad that I did it because it has felt like an important part of my grief journey."

Visiting the person who has died

It is during this time before the funeral that you may choose to spend some time with the person who has died.

This can be a difficult choice for some people and you may worry about making the wrong decision. Some people describe having had bad experiences of visiting people in the past, whereas others express regret for not having done so.

Every person, and every situation, is unique, and I can only suggest that you go with the decision which feels right to you and be kind to yourself.

You may not be able to articulate why you feel a certain way, and you don't have to – just do what you think is most helpful for you.

"I knew immediately that I wanted to spend as much time with her as I could. I knew that it was my last chance and I was going to take every possible opportunity to speak to her and be with her. I think it really helped me."

"I was with him when he died and I said my goodbye to his physical body then. I didn't feel that I needed to come and see him again."

"I had to go and check it was him and that he was being looked after properly. I knew it was him and I trusted the funeral director completely, but I just had to check."

If you do choose to spend time with the person who has died you may wish to see them, or you may just wish to be in the room with them with the coffin closed.

Either way, if the funeral director has not done so already, I would suggest that you ask them to describe the room and what you should expect when you go in. If you have a clearer image about what to expect then you may feel better prepared.

It is usual for the person who has died to feel cold. That doesn't mean that you can't touch them, but it can be upsetting if you are expecting someone to feel warm.

If there is anything that you would like the funeral director to change during the visit, then I would encourage you to ask them to do so.

Equally, if you have any questions about anything that you feel unsure about during the visit then the funeral director should be able to answer your questions; please don't hesitate to ask them.

Some people would like to visit once, and other people choose to visit regularly during the time before the funeral. It is up to you to decide what you feel would be most helpful.

You may find that your thoughts and feelings evolve during this time and that is not unusual. You are fully entitled to change your mind and should feel comfortable letting the funeral director know that the plan needs to change.

"At first, I thought that I didn't want to come to see her. But after a few days, my initial shock seemed to settle down and it suddenly seemed really important that I spend some time with her. In the end, I only went in for a few minutes, but I think I needed to see her to believe it had really happened, and I am glad I did."

Feelings and support

It is likely that there will be many people who would like to help you and show their support during this time. Some people are good at expressing this to you, whereas others may appear a little more awkward.

Asking people to run errands for you, cook you a fresh meal or cut the grass may give you one less thing to worry about and may be a huge privilege for them.

Many people have expectations about how they should feel after someone has died and the reality is often very different.

Some people expect to cope well because the death was expected and are then surprised at how upset they are, and others feel guilty when they appear to be dealing with the loss better than they expected to during the first few weeks and months.

I cannot stress enough that there is no right or wrong way to feel, and placing expectations about how you think you should feel is likely to do more harm than good.

If you can take each day and week at a time and try to identify what you find helpful at different times, then you are less likely to feel disappointed or frustrated when you don't feel exactly the way that you anticipated or predicted you would.

It is important to be kind to yourself and try to build in time to do things that help you to cope. We are all inherently very resilient, but we need different things to help to bring that resilience out.

Some people cope best by being busy, others prefer time alone, and most people need a mixture of the two.

Some people find exercise helpful and there may be certain family and friends who you enjoy being with. A gentleman I helped once said that the best thing to do was to go out and learn something new.

Everyone is different, and it might just take some time to work out what is most helpful for you at any given time.

If at any point you feel that you might benefit from some help then there are various sources of support available.

Some people would prefer to read a book or find information online whereas others would like to see a bereavement professional.

Some would rather seek support as an individual whereas others prefer to attend a group. Your funeral director, GP or local bereavement charity will be able to tell you what is available in your area and how you can access the support that is best for you.

Please use the boxes below to write down a few of your thoughts.

Are there any tasks that you feel might help you?

What are your current thoughts about personal care and spending time with the person who has died?

What are your current sources of support and how might you make sure that you look after yourself?

Chapter 9

After the service

Venue

After the funeral service (with or without the committal) has taken place, then you might like people to join you for some refreshments.

Again, this is not compulsory and some people would rather not arrange a formal gathering. If they want to, people can go for some informal refreshments afterwards and if the group is relatively small, a spontaneous plan can be made on the day depending on how people are feeling.

If you would prefer to plan refreshments in advance then you might like to invite people to a family home, or there are a wide range of alternative venues to choose from.

Earlier in the book, I suggested that you might like to decide on your preferred tone for the funeral, and this includes the refreshments afterwards.

Some people choose to give others the opportunity to join them for a relatively short gathering, whereas others see this time as an opportunity for people to share a few drinks and stories, and be together well into the evening.

Once this has been decided, it will help to guide you in all the decisions that you need to make thereafter.

"After the funeral I knew that I would rather go home and be by myself, but I knew that some people would be travelling quite far,

and it seemed rude to not offer them any refreshments. We arranged some teas and cakes in the church hall for afterwards and then I went home. I think some people stayed longer but I assume that they understood that I needed to get away."

"After the funeral service I wanted to spend time with friends and family. I wanted to have a few drinks and talk about Dad and be with people who loved him. For me it was the most helpful part of the day and I didn't really want it to end."

The choice of venue is likely to be influenced by the location of the service, number of guests, how far people are willing to travel and the type of venue that you prefer.

Some people feel that a relaxed pub is most suitable, whereas others like a hotel or restaurant venue. If the service is taking place in a church, then there may be an associated church hall or village hall close by.

Your funeral director will be able to suggest some venues close to the service location.

When you are considering your choice of venue, it is also helpful to decide whether you have any preferences as to how the room is laid out.

For example, would you prefer for most people to be standing and milling around or would you like people to be able to sit?

A combination of the two can also work very well, and you will of course need to be guided by the possibilities in the place that you have chosen.

If you would like to have a slide show, videos, or speeches with microphones, then you might like to ask whether the venue can accommodate these requests.

Refreshments

Once you have decided the venue, you may like to consider what refreshments you would like to be available there.

Some people prefer a simple afternoon tea or a cold buffet whereas others like a hot buffet or (less commonly) a sit-down meal. Most places can offer options from the simple to the more elaborate and will usually have some suggested menus for you to choose from.

It may also be worth considering whether any guests you are expecting have any specific dietary requirements, so you can ensure that the venue will cater for this in their preparations.

If you would like people to be able to have an alcoholic drink, then you will need to choose a venue with a bar or ask permission for you to bring some alcohol.

If the person who has died has a favourite tipple, then this can be a nice way to personalise the refreshments, but it can also quickly add cost to the funeral.

Some people decide to offer guests a drink on arrival, or have an open bar for the duration, but this is certainly not compulsory, and it would be unusual for this to be expected by guests.

"Nana loved a small sherry all year round, and we gave everyone a very small measure of sherry as they arrived. The church had kindly agreed that we could bring a few bottles into the church hall and I think Nana would have been delighted that everyone had a little toast to her in a place that was so important to her."

Some families choose to start the gathering with a toast to the person who has died. If it seems fitting to raise your glasses together in this way, then there may be a family member or friend who would be honoured to lead the toast.

If you wish, this could be the point at which people are given the opportunity to say a few words, if they would like to.

Some people choose to prepare refreshments themselves, or to involve others in this task. The preparations can become more manageable if people are delegated things to bring on the day, and people are often very pleased to have been asked and given the opportunity to be helpful. There are also many supermarkets or local providers where you could source some or all of the food and drink from.

Music and table arrangements

You may wish to have some music playing during the refreshments and most venues have the necessary equipment available for you to use.

Alternatively, you might prefer to not have any background noise, or you could choose to create a really uplifting atmosphere with a live band.

"He practised with his band every Wednesday night and I think it was one of the highlights of his week. I asked the other band members whether they would like to play a few songs during the wake and they were really pleased to be asked. It turned out really well."

You may like the flowers to be placed in the refreshment area for people to see or have small table arrangements made.

Personalised arrangements or table decorations can make the room look warmer and add a personal touch. Creating them can also give people the opportunity to contribute and be involved.

"She loved her china tea cups and saucers and her friends bought some from different charity shops and filled then with small posies of flowers to go on the tables. Afterwards, close friends were invited to take one home and I still have one sitting on the mantelpiece at my house."

A framed photograph, photo collage or projector with a photograph slide show can be placed in the room or personal memorabilia could be placed on a designated table.

If there were particular items like treasured collections of ornaments, medals, trophies or certificates then these could be placed on a display table for people to admire.

Similarly, if you have chosen to give people something to take away with them, these could be placed on a table with a sign instructing people to take one with them before they go.

Equally, if you would like people to contribute to a record of attendance or leave a memory or message then everything they need could be made available on a table in the venue.

As you can see, there are many ways to personalise the after-funeral refreshments, but it can be an equally meaningful gathering if people are just being together and showing love and support for one another.

Please use the boxes below to write down a few of your thoughts.

Do you have any thoughts about a venue for refreshments?

Is there a choice of food or drink that feels most appropriate?

What are your thoughts about music, layout or decorating the room?

Chapter 10

Post-funeral rituals

What is a post-funeral ritual?

A post-funeral ritual is anything that you do after the funeral, either as an individual or a group, which is organised or repeated and aims to commemorate or remember the person who has died.

There are many examples that could be included within this definition and they can provide a huge opportunity for meaning-making, memory creation and the development of continuing bonds.

For some people, these rituals may start immediately after the funeral, whereas others may not feel moved to do anything until sometime later.

Some people never engage in any post-funeral activities, whereas others describe them as even more helpful than the funeral itself.

As I mentioned previously, they also provide another opportunity to involve children in acknowledging that a loss has happened and to enable them to take part in acts of remembrance.

There are some rituals such as interring or scattering of ashes and erecting a headstone which are performed by many different people.

However, some individuals or families also create personal rituals of their own and here are some examples that people have kindly shared with me.

"We went back to the graveside the day after the funeral and sat a while. Everything

seems to happen so quickly on the day of the funeral and I didn't feel like I had spent the time there that I wanted to. I don't know how long I was there, but after some time I suddenly felt ready to go."

"Every Saturday I walk down to the bakery and buy a nice pastry. When the weather is fine, I sit on a bench in the park and enjoy my snack and when it is not, I take it home and sit by the window. He loved his sweet treats, and this way I feel close to him and remember the many lovely moments we had together."

"I found the process of emptying Mum's flat very difficult, but I think that it helped me to come to terms with what had happened. I felt really close to her and although I couldn't possibly keep everything, I kept her upright piano. Every time I play it I feel like she might be listening."

"Every year, on our sister's birthday, we all go out for a really fancy meal together. While she was alive she loved going out and always celebrated her birthday in style. The

evening is a very real mixture of sadness, gratitude and happiness, and I can't imagine that it will ever feel okay for her birthday to pass without us acknowledging it together in some way."

"My mother-in-law made the best chocolate cake in the world. She had given me the recipe before she died, and I now make it regularly. We always acknowledge that it is her cake, and we remember her while we eat it."

Ashes

Once the cremation has taken place, you can then decide what you would like to happen with the ashes.

There are different options for you to consider. Some are more traditional and others more unique, and I would suggest that you take some time before making your final choice.

There are many decisions that you have to make relatively quickly and giving yourself some time to reflect might be helpful at this point.

Some people feel strongly that all the ashes should stay together, whereas others prefer to split the ashes up and do several different things with them.

This can be especially helpful if people within the same family have differing opinions about what should be done.

"My sister really wanted to scatter some of Mum's ashes in her garden, whereas I thought that they should be buried with Dad. When we realised that we could do both it was a huge relief, because I'm not sure how else we could have resolved the situation."

Ashes can be returned to you from the crematorium in a container (usually plastic or cardboard) provided by the crematorium, or you could choose for a different container to be used.

Scatter tubes are cardboard tubes with a perforated top which enables ashes to be poured out relatively easily at the time of scattering. They come in a variety of colours and designs and can be personalised if you prefer.

Some people prefer to use an urn and there is a huge range of different designs and different urn materials available.

Metal, wood, wicker, wool, clay and many more options exist, and they range from the simple to the very elaborate.

I would suggest that you initially look at an urn catalogue, or search online, and once you have narrowed down the sort of style that you like, your funeral director should be able to help you to expand on your ideas.

Alternatively, many urn suppliers can be found online, and you could contact them directly if you prefer.

More and more alternatives to traditional urns are becoming available.

For example, you can buy large urns to be used as garden ornaments or in the shape of sundials, birdbaths or planters and Viking longboat urns can be set alight and placed into water.

Double urns are also available, enabling you to place two sets of ashes within one container.

"We chose a very pretty, natural-looking urn and it sits on our living room windowsill. I often speak to it and tell her what has been going on. I sometimes think the neighbours must worry about me talking to myself, but I have always told her what I am thinking so why should I stop now?"

You may choose to scatter all or some of the ashes at a favourite place or at the designated area in the crematorium.

The scattering could be accompanied by a ceremony led by an officiant, or you might plan a more informal gathering of family and close friends.

If you would like to scatter ashes in water, you might consider using a water-soluble urn designed specifically for this purpose.

When placed on the water, they float for a short while and then slowly sink down.

"A few months after the funeral, we gathered together to scatter her ashes. We all stood together and held hands and my sister read a poem that she had brought with her. Afterwards we all went for a drink and although it might sound a little strange, we all said that it was a really nice day."

It is possible to inter (bury) the ashes, perhaps with another member of the family who has died, or in a plot where other sets of ashes could be added at a later stage.

Plots to bury ashes are available in many church graveyards, cemeteries, natural and woodland burial grounds. At natural burial grounds a biodegradable ashes container must be used.

Again, the interment may have a ceremony associated with it, or you may choose to attend unaccompanied and place the ashes in the ground at the agreed time.

"We decided to bury his ashes in the local cemetery because it felt important to have a formal place that we could visit when we wanted to. We chose a very special headstone and I find myself going there often."

In addition to the possibilities mentioned above, there are many, many more choices available.

For example, there are small keepsakes, teddy bears and photo frames which contain a small amount of ashes within them.

Specialised pieces of jewellery can contain a small amount of ashes, or ashes can be turned into stones or diamonds. Ashes can be placed within fireworks, made into vinyl records or put in rockets and sent into space.

Listing all the possibilities would be overwhelming but if you are interested in finding out more then you could ask your funeral director to give you some guidance or alternatively, there is a huge amount of information available on the internet.

Crematorium

Most crematoria offer several possibilities to commemorate someone who has died.

You may wish to add their name to the book or scroll of remembrance, or you may have the opportunity to purchase a personalised plaque in the designated place in the crematorium.

In some crematoria it is possible to purchase a memorial bench within the grounds and your funeral director should be able to advise you about what is possible in your local area.

Memorial benches can also be purchased in a variety of other locations, such as in local beauty spots, public parks and village or town centres.

Headstones

A headstone can be erected over a grave six months after the burial has taken place, as it takes this amount of time for the ground to settle and to ensure that the headstone foundations will be secure enough.

Before that time, you are usually allowed to place a temporary cross or small stone on the grave, but this is not compulsory.

Your funeral director or people supporting you at the burial ground should be able to advise you about what is possible in the location that you have chosen.

Different burial grounds have different rules and regulations regarding headstones and these will need to be adhered to.

Often the monumental mason that you have chosen will have to seek permission in writing from whoever manages the burial ground before they start any work on the stone.

It can take some time for the headstone to be designed and created, so be aware that there may be a few months between choosing what you would like, and the stone being erected.

Your mason should be able to give you a clearer timescale because it is likely to depend on their workload and resources and this will fluctuate throughout the year.

Your funeral director or monumental mason should be able to tell you the range of headstone possibilities, which depends on the burial ground you have chosen.

They are likely to show you a catalogue of options, but you may also find it helpful to have a look round the burial ground and find some inspiration from the headstones already there.

Again, the internet can also be a helpful source because it can show you a much wider variety.

In addition to traditional monumental masons, there are also artists and sculptors who can help you to design a completely bespoke headstone and this service might be worth considering if you would like something more unique.

Your combined creativity will still need to comply with the burial ground rules, but they are certainly worth speaking to for you to explore what they can offer.

Broadly speaking, you will need to choose the type of stone, shape and inscription on the headstone. Different materials, for example granite, marble or Yorkshire stone look and feel different and this is often a helpful place to start.

Many cemeteries request that headstones are a fairly standardised shape because this looks neater and makes it easier to maintain the burial ground, whereas others are less restrictive.

Even if you have less control of the shape and size of the stone, you can usually add decorative engraving on the stone (for example, of a flower or significant symbol like a candle or heart) and you can choose how many flower holders, if any, you would like to be included on the base.

Choosing the words to be inscribed on the headstone can be an important decision for many people. Again, you could seek inspiration from other headstones at the cemetery, or on the internet.

If the grave is for more than one person, then it is usual to leave space on the stone for the second person's details to be added at a later stage.

The inscribed letters can usually be painted one of several different colours and your funeral director or mason will be able to tell you your options.

"We all met together to decide what should be written on Mum's headstone. I was worried that we might not agree because we have very different viewpoints on many things, but we managed to find some words that we all liked. I was surprised how

relieved I felt when we had worked so well together to do one last thing for Mum."

When the second interment is taking place in a grave, then the headstone will need to be removed and stored safely while the six-month period passes again.

During that time the headstone can be cleaned and repaired if needed and the new inscription can be added to the stone.

Some people find that they visit the graveside often, whereas others don't really feel compelled to return, and find other ways of being close to the person who has died.

Sometimes the reality is different to what you expect, and you may want to go more, or less, than you expected to.

Some people also describe that this has evolved for them over time, and it changes depending on what else is happening in their lives.

As I have said a few times in preceding chapters, I would encourage you to do what you feel is most helpful to you at the time, rather than being driven by the expectations that you, or others, have put on yourself.

We all experience grief in our own way and there is no right or wrong way to feel.

"I find myself popping in to see her at the cemetery quite a lot. It is on my route to and from work and when I have a few moments to spare I pull in and spend some time there. I never thought that I would want to visit at all!"

"It was important to Gran that she was buried in the cemetery close to her family and I know that she would have liked the headstone that we chose for her. I don't really like going there myself and prefer other ways of remembering her. Sometimes I worry that I ought to go anyway but then I remind myself that she always encouraged me to follow my heart, so I know that she would understand."

Fingerprints and locks of hair

For some people, keeping a lock of hair from the person who has died can be important and meaningful.

Although there are pieces of jewellery and decorative art that the hair can be incorporated into, many people just keep the hair somewhere safe.

If this is something that you would like, then you could take the lock or hair yourself or ask your funeral director to do so for you.

There are many different types of fingerprint, handprint and footprint jewellery and keepsakes available and some people find them very helpful and meaningful.

Fingerprints can be transferred onto pendants, charms, cufflinks and keyrings (amongst others) and can be enlarged so that they have a more textured feel.

Two sets of fingerprints can be joined together, names or phrases can be added, and more options are becoming available all the time.

"I wear his fingerprint necklace all the time. It is so very important to me and I like that I can touch it and feel the small grooves of the print. I don't think it is obvious to anyone who doesn't know me how significant an object it is, but it has given me great comfort."

A fingerprint necklace

It is also possible for a hand or foot print to be made into clay. It is possible for this to be made into a three-dimensional shape or imprinted into a clay board. Once made, the clay can be varnished or painted.

Again, if this is something that you think you would like then ask your funeral director to arrange for the print to be taken.

If this is something that you think you may find helpful now, or at some point in the future, then I would suggest asking your funeral director to take the fingerprints, handprints or footprints and keep them safe and available for you to use, should you choose to, in the future.

The print can always be destroyed at a later stage if you want to, but it will no longer be possible to take the print after the interment has taken place.

Although some people find these memorial options very helpful, some people either don't find it necessary or feel uncomfortable with the idea.

Both are perfectly valid perspectives and the important thing is that once you know what is possible, you can choose what is right for you.

Please use the boxes below to write down a few of your thoughts.

Do you have any current thoughts about ashes or headstones?

How do you feel about fingerprints, hand prints and locks of hair?

Has the chapter triggered any other thoughts?

Chapter 11

Final thoughts

Having come to the end of the book, I sincerely hope that you have gained a better understanding of funerals and funeral arranging and that many of your questions have been answered.

If you are considering your own choices or would like to have a conversation with someone close to you, I hope that you now have the information and inspiration that you need.

If you are anticipating that you will need to arrange a funeral soon or are just generally interested, then I hope that reading this book has made the process seem more accessible and you can now see how you can structure your thoughts and create a funeral that is meaningful and personal.

A funeral is an important human ritual and rite of passage, so I would encourage you to take your time and engage as much as you can to ensure that every funeral you are involved in is as helpful to you and your family and friends as possible.

With the right information, time and support, I sincerely hope that you can create a funeral that truly reflects the individual who has died and one that is right for you and yours.

Appendix 1

When someone dies at home

When someone dies at home then it is usual to call the doctor (GP) who has been caring for them to come out to confirm that they are happy for the person who has died to be brought into a funeral director's care.

If someone dies outside of normal working hours, then it may be an out-of-hours doctor who attends in their place.

In some cases, another healthcare professional (like a palliative care or district nurse) may attend instead and the doctor may not come at all. This is more common when someone has been receiving end-of-life care at home and their death has been expected.

To register the death, you will need the Medical Certificate of Cause of Death. This is a form which is completed by a doctor and can only be completed by someone who feels confident that they can determine the cause of death. They must also have seen the person who has died in the fourteen days prior to their death.

If the GP does not feel that they are able to complete this form, then they will need to refer to the coroner and await their instructions.

When someone dies at home, some friends and family would prefer for their loved one to move to the funeral service relatively quickly, whereas others would like to spend some time together at home first.

Some people prefer to see someone in their home environment after they have died, rather than somewhere that they are not familiar with.

Most funeral directors are available 24 hours a day, all year round and should be able to come to collect the person who has died as soon as the healthcare staff have confirmed that is allowed, and when you are ready for them to do so.

If you would like a funeral director to come to help you to care for the person who has died, in preparation for other people coming to see them, then the majority would be more than happy to do so.

Key points:

- A healthcare professional will need to attend to confirm the funeral director can bring the person into their care

- If you would like to look after the person who has died at home for a short while, then a funeral director can help you to do so

- The funeral director can attend 24/7

- A doctor will need to complete a Medical Certificate of Cause of Death and if they are unable to do so, the coroner will need to be consulted

Appendix 2

When someone dies in professional care

In a hospital, hospice, nursing or residential care home, the staff who have cared for the person who has died will know what to do next.

You will also find they will offer you practical advice and support after the death and hospitals have dedicated bereavement liaison teams who will help you as much as they can.

If the person who has died is in hospital, they will be taken to the hospital mortuary after they have died. Some hospices and nursing homes have a small mortuary or other specific room where they care for people once they have died, or they may leave the individual in their room or bay.

When someone dies in hospital or a hospice then a doctor will be called to confirm whether a Medical Certificate of Cause of Death will be issued.

If this is not possible then the death will need to be referred to the coroner and the death cannot be registered (or funeral arrangements confirmed) until the coroner has completed their enquiries.

Nursing homes will either contact the local (or on-call) GP, or members of the nursing team may be specifically trained to decide whether it is appropriate for the person who has died to be brought into the care of the funeral director.

Most hospital mortuaries will allow the individual to be collected by the funeral director only after the death has been registered.

Similarly, if the person has chosen to be cremated then members of hospital staff will need to complete some additional, cremation-specific paperwork and the funeral director may not be allowed to attend until this has been completed.

At the moment, there is a charge for this paperwork, but this may change in the future.

Most families and friends request that the person who has died be moved into the funeral director's care as soon as possible.

Having said that, it is likely to be possible to spend some time together in the place where they have died, or you may wish to see whether they can return home for a time. In some circumstances this may not be possible.

Key points:

- The staff will be able to give you guidance about what will happen next

- Nursing homes and hospices have different facilities and procedures about when the person who has died can be brought into a funeral director's care

- If you would like to spend some time with the person who has died in the place where they died, then the staff will do everything they can to help you to do so

- Someone is usually only able to leave the hospital once their death has been registered and, if applicable, cremation-specific paperwork has been completed

Appendix 3

Sudden or unexpected death

When someone dies unexpectedly at home or in residential or nursing care, it is usual for the ambulance service to attend first.

If they confirm that the person has died and there is nothing more that they can do, then they would usually call the police.

The police will then liaise with the coroner, and the person who has died will be collected by either a funeral director commissioned by the coroner to provide transport, or by a funeral director of your choice.

Depending on the circumstances, the individual will be brought either to the funeral director's premises, or to the mortuary specified by the coroner.

If someone dies unexpectedly in hospital, then the coroner will also need to be informed.

Similarly, the coroner will need to be consulted if someone dies in a public place or if there is any suspicion that the death may have been violent or unnatural.

Once the coroner is involved, it is their responsibility to establish the cause of death.

In some cases, the coroner may decide that they do not need to take any further action and may request that the hospital doctor or GP issues the Medical Certificate of Cause of Death.

In other cases, the coroner may decide that a post mortem (autopsy) needs to be completed. They will then also decide whether they will need to open an inquest or not.

The coroner is working in your interests and will keep you informed throughout. If you would like your funeral director to support you by contacting the coroner's officers on your behalf then please ask them to do so.

Even if the coroner is involved and this is likely to cause some uncertainty and delay, I would still encourage you to contact a funeral director as soon as possible so that you can start to discuss your thoughts and explore some possibilities.

If the person who has died has been brought to a funeral director that you have not chosen yourself then you are free to engage the services of another funeral director instead (and you should not incur any charges).

Particularly when someone has died suddenly, you may have given very little thought to what sort of funeral would best reflect the life of the individual who has died and having some extra time may be beneficial.

Key points:

- The coroner will need to be involved when a death is unexpected, sudden, in public or if there are any concerns that it may be due to violent or unnatural causes

- The coroner's officers will keep you informed throughout the process and your funeral director can also give you guidance and support

- You can choose to be supported by any funeral director that you want to and are not obliged to use the funeral service who has been appointed by the coroner to provide transport

- You may wish to meet with the funeral director sooner, rather than later. Although you will not be able to finalise any arrangements immediately, it will give you more time to consider your options and gather your thoughts.

Appendix 4

Dying abroad and returning to England

When someone dies abroad it is often unexpected and can be a particularly difficult and confusing time for family and friends.

The death may have occurred in a country where people speak a different language and there are often unfamiliar procedures that need to be adhered to.

In some cases, many costs are covered by valid travel insurance but in other situations you may be responsible for paying for repatriation.

The costs can be significant, and I would suggest that you make sure that people are clear with you about the costs of any service they are offering.

If an English resident has died abroad then the death must be registered abroad, in accordance with local policy.

This can only occur once a Medical Certificate of Cause of Death has been issued by local medical staff or a local coroner.

It is possible to also register the death with the British Consulate abroad and to request a British death certificate (for which there may be a significant charge).

This is not compulsory and a foreign certificate confirming that the death has been registered abroad is recognised by all the necessary British organisations (like banks etc.).

Funerals Your Way

It is possible to arrange for a burial or cremation to take place abroad with the support of the British Consulate and a local funeral director.

If cremation has taken place abroad then you may wish to bring the ashes back home.

Alternatively, you may wish for burial or cremation to take place at home and in that case, the British Consulate and a local funeral director abroad will support you to arrange for you and your loved one to return home.

In this case you will need to ask a funeral director in England to support you by liaising with a local funeral director abroad, British Consulate staff, your travel insurance company and airlines.

They could arrange to meet you and the person who has died immediately upon return to England and then support you with the remainder of the funeral arranging process.

Key points:

- There are several people who can support you when someone dies abroad

- Repatriation can be very expensive so ask for all costs in advance

- If you engage a local funeral director in England to support you, then they will help you to liaise with the various authorities and meet you and the person who has died upon return to England

Appendix 5

Registering a death

In most cases, a death should be registered in the district where the person died, and currently this should occur within 5 days.

However, there will be some occasions where this is not possible, for example if it takes some time for the Medical Certificate of Death to be obtained. In this case the registrar will likely give permission for a 14 days extension.

A family member would usually meet with the registrar and they must have the

Medical Certificate of Cause of Death to do so. In most cases you need to make an appointment to see the registrar in person and can only make this appointment when you have the relevant paperwork.

However, in some areas, the hospital bereavement team will arrange this appointment for you (to take place at the hospital) and this means that you can see the registrar while you collect the Medical Certificate of Cause of Death.

To complete the registration process you also need to know the full name, main address and the date of birth of the person who has died.

Whoever meets the registrar should also know the details of the date and place of death.

Ideally, the registrar would also like to know the individual's occupation, whether they were receiving any state benefits at the time of their death and, if they were married, the name and date of birth of the surviving widow or widower.

Once this information has been provided and the death has been registered, you will be given:

- Death certificate – green form to be handed to the funeral director

- DWP form and contact details – which gives information relating to any benefits received

- Tell Us Once information and unique reference number – see below

The registrar will provide you with the death certificate and extra copies can be purchased from the registrar. Copies are likely to be required if you are dealing with the financial affairs of the person who has died.

Many authorities have a 'Tell Us Once' service which allows you to inform a number of government departments about a death in one go. It is a free and optional service which is available once you have registered the death with the registrar. You will be given a unique reference number to use, either online or by telephone, which confirms the death has been registered.

With this information, 'Tell Us Once' will then inform:

- HMRC – to organise tax and benefit cancellation
- DWP – to cancel benefits
- Passport Office
- DVLA
- Local council – to cancel housing benefit, council tax information, blue badge and to remove from the electoral register
- Public sector / Armed Forces – to organise pensions being paid or being paid into

Appendix 6

Funeral costs explained

Funerals can be very expensive and can place individuals and families under significant financial pressure and stress.

It is always worth bearing in mind that when presented with a funeral invoice, many banks will pay the funeral expenses directly from the bank account of the person who has died (assuming there are enough funds available).

Different funeral directors have different policies about when they require payment and many request a deposit before the funeral takes place (usually to cover the disbursement fees explained below).

Some funeral directors will await payment until probate has been completed but you should not assume this is the case. If this is an important consideration for you then I would suggest that you establish whether a funeral director's terms are acceptable to you, before you finally decide to work with them.

Understanding funeral costs will help you to make the decisions that are right for you during the planning process and will enable you to identify where you feel your money is best spent.

Funeral directors have various ways of dividing the costs of a funeral but one way to consider them is as a combination of:

1. Funeral director's (professional) fees

2. Ancillary or discretionary costs

3. Disbursements

Funeral director's (professional) fees

These are the costs paid to the funeral director for their time and support with the funeral.

Usually this fee includes bringing the person who has died into the funeral director's care, caring for the person who has died, spending time with you and with other professionals, arranging the service, and the coordinating and directing of the funeral on the day. It also includes use of their premises to spend time with the person who has died.

Ancillary or discretionary costs

These will vary from funeral to funeral and are dependent on your own personal preferences. These include coffin choice, vehicles, flower selection, any memorial items and keepsakes or ashes urns.

These will be decided during the funeral planning process and then the funeral director will generally arrange them on your behalf.

Disbursements

These are unavoidable costs that must be paid to other people involved in the funeral.

This will include costs for medical certificates, cremation or burial (including the cost of the plot and digging the grave) and other costs relating to the funeral service.

These costs are set locally and the funeral director does not have any control over them. The funeral director generally pays them on your behalf and then includes them on the final invoice.

Appendix 8

Green funerals

People are increasingly concerned about the impact that they have on the world we live in.

Some may wish to have a completely "green" funeral, whereas others may wish merely to incorporate some environmentally friendly elements.

A funeral is often a time for reflection and including "greener" options can be a powerful signal to those present.

Choosing a coffin made from biodegradable materials (such as cardboard, willow or bamboo) is a common way to minimise your impact on the environment.

However, it is also important to know how far these coffins have travelled as more locally grown and manufactured options may be preferable.

If you would prefer a wooden (or wood effect) coffin, then there are still greener choices such as locally sourced hardwoods like oak or cherry and softwoods like pine. Manufacturers will be able to advise where the wood has been grown and whether it is Forest Stewardship Council (FSC) registered.

Burial, compared to cremation, is generally regarded to be a greener choice as it avoids the mercury, dioxin and carbon monoxide emissions associated with cremation.

Furthermore, burial closer to the surface (such as in a natural burial ground) means that decomposition is aerobic and is more beneficial for the environment.

You may wish to consider how far the body and the guests travel and the type of fuel used in transportation.

Choosing a local burial ground and having the service in the same location may be possible and you may wish to consider using an electric hearse (if it is available where you are).

Guests can be encouraged to share cars or travel together in a larger vehicle.

There are several other things to consider when contemplating making greener choices.

You might like to ensure that flowers are sourced locally or handpicked from your own garden so that they haven't travelled too far to reach their final destination. It is also possible to avoid the use of cellophane and only use natural materials in floral arrangements.

Finally, use of paper can be minimised by not using written Order of Service booklets, asking people to share them or using recycled paper for them to be printed on.

Key points:

- You may wish to include some more environmentally friendly funeral choices

- A wide range of choices are still available

- Simple alternatives and changes can have a large impact

Appendix 9

Funerals in the digital age

We live in a time where technology is a huge part of our everyday lives and these advances have had an impact on funerals too.

Firstly, there are many online resources to help you to understand your funeral choices, express your wishes and purchase online funeral plans.

When someone dies, this is now regularly communicated online and via social media and it is not uncommon for someone to find out online that someone they know is dying or has died.

There are a range of different websites which try to help you to compare and choose a funeral director. At the moment, these comparisons are mainly on price, rather than on quality or value for money.

Funeral director services are increasingly being reviewed online and this information is readily available to help you to decide which funeral director you would like to use.

Information about local venues, committal locations, coffins, flowers and much more can be found online, and this can be a very powerful source of information.

People use technology to communicate ideas with each other and to disseminate details about the funeral to family and friends far and wide.

On the day of the funeral, photograph slide shows, videos and live-streaming of the funeral are increasingly common, and donations are often collected online.

Dedicated memorial websites are available giving people the opportunity to communicate details about the funeral and welcome people to share memories or photographs, write messages, light virtual candles and make donations in memory of the person who has died.

Digital condolence books and personalised photo albums are available and as most people are now able to take photographs and videos on their phones while at funerals, this is also becoming more common.

Many people seem to find having these images meaningful and reassuring and the stigma of taking photos at funerals seems to be rapidly declining.

There is also a huge range of bereavement advice and support available online and through social media.

People can communicate with others who are geographically very far away (and can do so relatively anonymously) and a huge range of bereavement and grief networks are highly accessible to many.

As advances in artificial intelligence and virtual and augmented reality continue, these changes are likely to also have an impact on the way that people are supported to create and experience funerals.

Key points:

- Technology can play an important part in planning and experiencing funerals

- Well placed technology can be very helpful and empowering, and I suggest that you choose the technology that you feel best meets your needs

Printed in Great Britain
by Amazon